Book Description

Although Buddhists, Chinese and other religions from the ancient Middle East may have practiced these techniques centuries ago, they are rapidly becoming mainstream practices in the western world today. There is a distinctive link between mindfulness and meditation where there are benefits to be enjoyed daily, way too many for these ancient art forms to be ignored.

The secret to beginning to master this practice lies in awareness, living in the moment, learning to understand your feelings and emotions. It's also knowing how the environment influences us, and discovering how to be mindful in each situation of our lives.

This book will teach you how to develop awareness of self and others, compassion, empathy, how to stop judging yourself or expecting perfection. It will help you develop the tools you need not just for today but long-term.

You can reduce stress and anxiety in your life, learn how to use mindful meditation to improve your day, visualize the things that you want, and let go of the things holding you back. Allow the universe or that higher power to take control and lead you to peace and happiness.

Discover each of these things and much more, it's easier than you think. Once you understand the principles behind meditation and mindfulness you tap into your inner self to benefit every area of your life.

Meditation & Mindfulness

A Quick Guide to Learning the Art of Mindfulness - Includes Guided Meditations

Noah M. Worrall

© Copyright 2022 - All rights reserved.

The content contained within this book may not be reproduced, duplicated, or transmitted without direct written permission from the author or the publisher.

Under no circumstances will any blame or legal responsibility be held against the publisher, or author, for any damages, reparation, or monetary loss due to the information contained within this book, either directly or indirectly.

Legal Notice:

This book is copyright protected. It is only for personal use. You cannot amend, distribute, sell, use, quote, or paraphrase any part, or the content within this book, without the consent of the author or publisher.

Disclaimer Notice:

Please note the information contained within this document is for educational and entertainment purposes only. All effort has been executed to present accurate, up-to-date, reliable, complete information. No warranties of any kind are declared or implied. Readers acknowledge that the author is not engaged in the rendering of legal, financial, medical, or professional advice. The content within this book has been derived from various sources. Please consult a licensed professional before attempting any techniques outlined in this book.

By reading this document, the reader agrees that under no circumstances is the author responsible for any losses, direct or indirect, that are incurred as a result of the use of the information contained within this document, including, but not limited to, errors, omissions, or inaccuracies.

Table of Contents

Book Description

Table of Contents

Introduction

   About the author

Chapter 1: The History of Meditation & Mindfulness

   History of Meditation

   The History of Mindfulness

   The Difference Between Meditation & Mindfulness

   How Meditation & Mindfulness Complement One Another

Chapter 2: The Science Behind Meditation & Mindfulness

   Reasons Why Meditation and Mindfulness Improves Your Life

   What Illnesses Can it Help With?

   Positive State of Mind

   Live in the Now and Not in the Past

   Stages of Meditation

Chapter 3: The Motivation Behind Meditation & Mindfulness

   Motivations to Meditate

   Reasons for meditation

Understanding Mindfulness

Chapter 4: Learning the Art of Practice

What is Practice and Why you should

Body scan

Breathing exercises

Relaxation

Visualization

The best time of day

Start small

Basic techniques

Intermediate techniques

Advanced techniques

Accept that it may take time

Don't feel bad if you get bored or fall asleep

Chapter 5: How Meditation & Mindfulness Benefit Us All

Us and them

Other benefits

Chapter 6: The Importance of a Daily Routine

Why meditation should be part of your daily routine

Tips to create positive habits

Benefits of looking forward to "ME" time

Chapter 7: Guided Meditations

Before you begin

Mindfulness meditation

Beginning of Mindfulness Meditation

Breathing

Check in with Your Body

Closing Your Meditation

Breathing – and counting your breath exercise

Preparation Before You Begin

Beginning of Breathing Meditation

Check in with Your Body

Closing Your Meditation

Walking meditation

Preparation Before You Begin

Beginning of Walking Meditation

Check in with Your Body

Closing Your Meditation

Visualization meditation

Preparation Before You Begin

Breathing

Beginning of Your Visualization Meditation

- Check in with Your Body
- Closing Your Meditation
- Sleep meditation
  - Preparation Before You Begin
  - Breathing
  - Check in with Your Body
  - Closing Your Meditation
- Conclusion
- Resources
- References

"When your world moves too fast and you lose yourself in the chaos, introduce yourself to each color of the sunset. Reacquaint yourself with the earth beneath your feet. Thank the air that surrounds you with every breath you take. Find yourself in the appreciation of life."

~ Christy Ann Martine (Martine, 2019)

Introduction

"Place your hands into soil to feel grounded. Wade into water to feel emotionally healed. Fill your lungs with fresh air to feel mentally clear. Raise your face to the heat of the sun and connect with that fire to feel your own immense power."

~ Victoria Erickson, Rebelle Society (GoodTherapy.org Staff, 2018)

In 2020 the American Psychological Association (APA) reported that nearly two in three people were suffering from some form of stress related issues. This means 65% of the population could be experiencing anything from basic anxiety all the way through to devastating, debilitating levels of depression. In both instances one of the main solutions recommended by the medical profession is through chronic medication. (American Psychological Association, 2020)

What about those of us that don't want to go down that route? Finding workable solutions to quiet the mind and body in a world that is constantly spinning at a maddening pace is not easy. Necessary, but not something that can be achieved without a practical, workable guideline of some description.

Are you tired? This is not simply a physical question. Although yes, our body's become physically exhausted when we don't have the coping mechanisms to process daily stressors. The fatigue I'm referring to is so much more... It is mental, emotional, psychological, and physiological. It is not knowing what to do when you are pressurized by never-ending deadlines, and meetings in the workplace. It is not knowing how to be everything you feel you need to be for your family.

Do you feel like you are constantly losing the battle against those demons that haunt you because you aren't always present—even when you are. Are you looking for ways to turn off the madness? Quieten the voices in your head. Gain control over all those thoughts that seem to be running rampant!

If you are anything like me then having a basic understanding of what things are about is important. Before we dive into ways meditation and mindfulness can add value to your life you need to know a bit more about why it is going to help you. How is it going to lead you to discovering that inner peace and calm you crave, and why should you trust it? My goal is to make this journey of discovery as simple as possible.

The aim is for *Meditation & Mindfulness: A Quick Guide to Learning the Art of Mindfulness* to be a useful tool that can make a genuine difference in your life. Providing you with practical applications that you can use immediately. Applications that can make a genuine difference in your life.

A resource you will keep coming back to time and time again. One that becomes a daily companion to the meditation and mindfulness process you decide to adopt as your own. My message is simple, guided meditation and mindfulness doesn't need to be complicated. You don't need to have any special abilities or equipment. All you need is a solution with ways to deal with the day-to-day challenges that life is constantly throwing in your direction.

If you are under constant pressure and have difficulty in finding the perfect work/life balance then this resource is for you. The chapters that follow will give you a brief insight into both mindfulness and meditation. Their origins and why they are so effective in providing relief. Calming the mind and speaking peace to the soul.

The world will continue to become even more chaotic as time goes by. There's no stopping daily challenges and pressures. The majority of external pressures you experience in your life are out of your control. The one thing you do have control over however is how you respond to these events.

Once you have a clear guideline, a roadmap so to speak. Once you have the skills and knowledge necessary, you can make your life journey one filled with a calmer, happier, and more peaceful life.

The strategies in the pages that follow are simple.

Learning to control your thoughts and quieten your mind is possible.

Finding ways to live in the moment without regrets is part of the solution.

Implementing what I'm going to share with you is much easier than you think. There are effective ways of being able to calm your mind that seems to be spiraling out of control. Move past those emotions that are keeping you stuck. Stuck in the past, or the present. Using guided meditation and mindfulness is simple, safe, and non-addictive. Unless you currently crave peace and harmony in your life.

Meditation & Mindfulness: A Quick Guide to Learning the Art of Mindfulness offers you ways to deal with daily challenges. There are a range of guided meditations to help almost any life experience you may be faced with. As an added bonus, I have included a wealth of useful resources for you to continue on your road to a healthier, happier life. One filled with the inner peace you've been searching for.

About the author

Throughout his youth and even now confidence has always been something the author has battled with. Nobody would have guessed it as a young boy because his lack of confidence was always masked. Hidden behind sport and a wide circle of friends.

His shyness was so severe that panic attacks were a constant companion. None of these emotions and challenges were ever shared with anyone. For a long time he doubted himself and his abilities. He felt that somehow he was flawed and an inferiority complex of monumental proportions crept into his life that was all-consuming.

If you had to ask any of his friends, co-workers, or family to describe him today they will say the exact opposite is true. They will describe him as being an extremely confident, successful business owner who is loyal, and sensitive to the needs of others. Deep down the constant struggle with low self-esteem and almost non-existent confidence levels was and is still something he faces each day. The difference being that today he knows what he needs to do to keep these emotions under control.

The tools that made it possible for him to move through school, and even now, can be traced back to meditation and mindfulness. He learned to make use of breathing techniques to calm his mind, long before he even knew what it was and how beneficial this application could be in all areas of his life.

Despite the fake persona the world saw, struggles with lack of confidence, severe anxiety, and inferiority were relentless.

Being actively involved in sport provided some relief and so it made sense to him that to feel normal he needed to become the best. He would excel at basketball and other sports throughout school and beyond, all the while keeping his sense of inferiority well hidden. When asked to describe this further his response would be "We all have our own demons. It is part of our make-up. Part of who we are."

Leaving a distinguished career in law-enforcement he ventured into his own business to share what he has discovered about meditation and mindfulness. This has been a journey for more than two decades. He realized that personal development and self-help was the environment he was passionate about and one he had been searching for. Within this niche he has spent the last 20 years working with businesses, mindfulness coaches and fully immersed in this field. His focus has not only been working with the formal corporate environment but he has spent time working with children, teaching them to make use of these tools. Something he never had while growing up.

Learning and absorbing as much information on mindfulness and meditation taught him which tools were most effective and how adopting each of these positive actions and turning them into habits results in the power to turn your whole life around. It all starts with meditation and mindfulness. He can pass on the insight he has gained over 20 years because he has been using these selfsame techniques daily to keep the present moment at the front of his mind constantly. Implementing these solutions has helped his own confidence levels grow exponentially.

Meditation and Mindfulness have been such a great part in Noah's life and his success. He is convinced that it is thanks to these skills and techniques that he is where he is today.

His reason for writing this book is to share his knowledge, experience, and the simplicity in adopting these principles into your life. It is his goal to help others learn to achieve calm amidst the chaos of the world. Through mindfulness goals can be achieved, even for younger individuals.

These techniques can be applied universally to all areas of one's life. Whether it happens to be in sport, professionally as a business owner or employee. They can assist in relationships with your spouse, partner, children, extended family members as well as those that cross your path. In short, his message is clear. Anything is possible if you believe it to be.

Noah is happily married with two sons. As a first-time author, his vision for the chapters that follow is to share how your life can be transformed through small and simple adjustments to things you do each day. It is his goal to reach and help as many people as possible who may think that all is lost, when genuine solutions are readily available. All you need is to really want it bad enough.

Chapter 1: The History of Meditation & Mindfulness

"The goal of meditation is not to get rid of thoughts or emotions. The goal is to become more aware of your thoughts and emotions and learn how to move through them without getting stuck."

~ Dr. P. Goldin (Shaw, 2019)

Before getting into how meditation and mindfulness can make a difference in your life, you need to understand a little more about its history, where each has come from as well as reasons why they have become such new-age phenomena again. Before taking this journey with me it should also be mentioned that there are so many benefits to incorporating these two positive methodologies to your life. This will be the main focus in Chapter 5 but some of the basic benefits are worth mentioning here.

History of Meditation

While society would have you believe that meditation has only been around for the last couple of decades, being made popular by new-age personal development icons, this is far from the truth. Instead of just decades, try looking at centuries instead. Between meditation and mindfulness, they are some of the oldest techniques available. The earliest use of meditation has been part of religion for centuries.

Because so many religions can lay claim to using meditation as part of their beliefs, as the religion has evolved over time to meet the ever-increasing needs of the modern world, meditation has changed as well. With correct application, these techniques can provide the answers to those things we suffer from thanks to ever-increasing stressors and demands on our lives.

It is quite possible that never in the history of the world has there been a greater need for the benefits that meditation has to offer. Just over the last few years there has been a steep increase in what you might refer to as modern diseases resulting from the turmoil the world is currently in. Things that we are really battling with are anxiety, stress, and depression. There's a desperate need to find something that works, something that you aren't going to have to become addicted to, something that is going to bring you instant relief and it's not going to put you into a hole financially.

By using the techniques I am going to discuss in the following chapters, you will discover ways to quieten your mind, which will benefit your mental health, easing tensions that accompany the stress I referred to above. Just learning to manage these modern diseases can help you find inner peace daily. You would think that these are surely mental disorders rather than diseases? The acceptable definition of the word "disease" is a disorder, condition, illness, or abnormality. Being under constant stress or battling bouts of depression that you simply cannot seem to shake meets the above criteria of this definition.

The root word for "meditation" is Latin. "*Meditari*" means to contemplate, think, and reflect on something. Looking at it logically today it is easy to identify these roots in what we currently refer to as Yoga. The main aim of this popular form of exercise is for the mind to become focused. To tap into our spiritual awareness. Because the earliest forms of meditation, or Yoga Sutras haven't been documented, or at least no records have survived, archeologists think that people have been practicing this way of life since about 5,000 B.C.

While texts were only discovered around 1,500 BCE that seem to indicate that it had been around for centuries before it was adopted and practiced by the Hindu religion. Wall art with pictures of individuals in poses that are now linked to meditation were discovered in India and archeologists believe these date back to 5,000 BCE.

China, and India are mentioned in texts from 500 BCE referring to other religions such as the Buddhists and Taoists. It would take a number of centuries before Bhagavad Gita would pen philosophical documents that explained how yoga and meditation could help those practicing both in combination with each other would result in being able to live on a life that was on a much higher spiritual plane.

By 400 B.C. a scholar of yoga, Patanjali, wrote what has become widely known as The Yoga Sutras. Consisting of nine different stages, the eighth stage was "meditation."

Thanks to the Egyptians, the practice of yoga became more popular when a philosopher discussed exercises to focus the mind. Each of these had a religious component.

Plato added to these although it was only really recorded in the Hebrew bible that the Jews were avid believers of meditation and this was a large part of the Jewish faith.

The east adopted meditation when a Japanese Buddhist monk, Dosho, was the first to dedicate an entire area (room) just for meditation. This was in 1227. This became known as Zen Buddhism.

The middle ages saw the inclusion of many meditative practices as part of the Kabbalah and the Jewish Torah. Islam adopted it as part of their mysticism. You might say that this was part of the middle ages.

During the Byzantine era, the Greeks highlighted biblical texts that could be repeated while breathing.

By the 18th century, the study of Buddhism for the purpose of meditation was adopted for the first time in the west. Thanks to a book dedicated to the spiritual journey of self-discover, Siddharta, first published in 1922. Shortly after, the *Book of the Dead* appeared (n.d.). Written by a Tibetan, this was the first book to be published in English. Meditation, as mentioned in this book, was focused on self-improvement, relaxation techniques, and reducing levels of stress. It never really focused on religion at all. It was around this time that medical professionals began to actively research the effects and benefits of meditation both mentally and physically.

Harvard University would become the first institution to formally recognize that both medicine and spirituality could be combined to impact the mind and body simultaneously. This was studied in-depth by Dr. Herbert Benson who would become the very first professor of what was known as "mind, body medicine." This was first taught at Harvard's school of medicine. The west would begin to adopt these practices on a serious basis.

Jon Kabat-Zinn would create a clinic dedicated to stress reduction using meditation. Deepak Chopra, a center for well-being. These are two well-known names in the field of what is also known as oriental philosophy. From east to west, spanning thousands of years, meditation would finally become a mainstream practice across the globe.

The History of Mindfulness

Mindfulness has been around for just as long as meditation, the reality is that it was never really given a name until more recently. This is also because it has become more popular as a means of improving well-being, restoring calm, slowing down, and observing things happening around you. It is as though mindfulness is continuing to evolve.

The first recorded use of mindfulness practices are linked to Hinduism and the practice of yoga. This dates back as far as between 2,300, and 1,500 BCE. Its roots lead back to what is currently referred to as Pakistan.

In Sanskrit, the word for remembering is "smriti." The belief behind this is to remind ourselves to be present. We can become aware of all things around us. It is enlightenment.

In Hindu, the word "Dhyāna" refers to contemplation. Silence and acceptance. Although part of meditation, this is really what is at the heart of mindfulness. It's where the mind can become focused to the point where everything else in the background disappears. Although it may be described as meditation, it is all done consciously.

Indian roots of mindfulness can be traced as far back as the Vedic age, approximately 1,500 to 1,100 BCE. This period is well documented through the Vedas, a form of Vedic literature. These documents clearly refer to mindfulness as part of Buddhist practices. The reason for including mindfulness to meditation rituals was to help them reach Nirvana. To Buddhists, this is a state where they believe enlightenment is achieved. Unconditional, lasting happiness.

Part of this process has been mastering the art of peeling away layers of consciousness. Mindfulness can be used to strip away negative thinking and judgment. All the things that fill the mind with 'stuff' that is really unimportant.

The Buddhist link is more than just that awareness of things taking place in the moment. To practicing Buddhists, this awareness is the first step necessary to achieve enlightenment.

Practiced for centuries by Buddhists. The term "mindfulness" is closely described as being connected to the Buddhist word "Sati." A direct translation of this term refers to being aware of things from moment to moment. Siddhārtha Gautama was referred to as the original Buddha and founder of the religious movement around the fifth century BCE.

Similar to the extended period of meditation in the east before making its way to the west, mindfulness was exactly the same. The first mention of mindfulness in the west was during the 1970s. John Kabat-Zinn is believed to have introduced it in his Stress Reduction Clinic in 1979. This clinic was attached to the University of Massachusetts' Medical School. Kabat-Zinn developed a program that would be known as "Mindfulness-Based Stress Reduction." This almost severed the close ties between Buddhism and mindfulness, pulling it more into the scientific sphere. Because of his earlier practices of mindfulness and introduction of the principles to the west, he has long been recognized as the father of modern mindfulness in the western world.

The big question was whether the west was actually ready for the full-blown practice of the art of mindfulness and meditation, or whether it needed to be adapted to suit the application. This is exactly what Kabat-Zinn did. As he introduced these practices into the medical industry the links with mysticism and each of the eastern cultures became diluted. He would avoid any terminology that could link it to Buddhism.

Given that this was the 1970s, it was the era of all things 'hippie.' He knew he would not be able to pass this off to his medical patients unless he adapted the application, changed terminology, and basically repackaged it to meet the needs of his patients. In his own words he describes how he changed mindfulness from what it was originally, to tie into his mindfulness-based program,

> I bent over backward to structure it and find ways to speak about it that avoided as much as possible the risk of it being seen as Buddhist, New Age, Eastern mysticism, or just plain flaky. (Okafor, 2022)

This would not always have to remain in the shadows however, the more successful his program became and the more people he was able to treat and to help, the more empirical data he was able to gather, firmly cementing the effectiveness of mindfulness and meditation in modern-day healing.

In 1990 he published a book entitled *Full Catastrophe Living.* (Kabat-Zinn, 2008). It was only after this publication that mindfulness and meditation began to grow. Still very much linked to helping reduce stress for those diagnosed with and suffering from mental health related illnesses. This technique was applied as a coping method for anxiety, stress, and even depression.

Like meditation, mindfulness is not only linked to Buddhism. It was practiced by many ancient religions. Most referred to it as "living in the moment." Being present in the now. Some of these religions include Hinduism, Muslim, and even beliefs in Judaism, as well as Christianity. Think for a moment about ancient meditation techniques and practices that have been around for centuries. Practices like Tai Chi. Yoga is another form of meditation that incorporates mindfulness as part of its beliefs. Although it may have started with religious roots, this is certainly not where it has stayed.

Modern-day users see it as being able to raise awareness. Although becoming more mainstream there are still direct links to practicing various forms of mindfulness in each religion out there.

Christianity refers to the spirit as being central to our link with deity. According to Eckhart Tolle, "Some Christian mystics have called it the Christ within." In his book, *Practicing the Presence of God*, the author refers to awareness of the 'Holy Spirit.' (Lawrence, 2018).

Muslims refer to a constant awareness that they are under the constant eye of Allah. They firmly believe that we are all born with this purity of heart irrespective of circumstance. A belief also held by many Christian religions. For Muslims they practice accessing this power through mindfulness.

The Difference Between Meditation & Mindfulness

Many mistakenly believe that meditation and mindfulness are exactly the same thing. According to Jon Kabat-Zinn, as quoted in Ed and Deb Shapiro's book, *The Unexpected Power of Mindfulness Meditation (2019)*, "Mindfulness is the awareness that arises when we non-judgmentally pay attention in the present moment. It cultivates access to core aspects of our own minds and bodies that our very sanity depends on." They further go on to say that,

> Mindfulness, which includes tenderness and kindness toward ourselves, restores dimensions of our being. These have never actually been missing, just that we have been missing them, we have been absorbed elsewhere. When your mind clarifies and opens, your heart also clarifies and opens. (Shapiro & Shapiro, 2019).

Although opposite to one another, mindfulness and meditation are still inextricably linked together. Meditation is supported by mindfulness whereas mindfulness is expanded by meditation. You can practice mindfulness at any time of the day, in any given situation. It usually doesn't take a very long time and just a few minutes can restore a sense of peace and calm to your mind. Meditation on the other hand usually requires a set amount of time to be effective. Think about doing a Tai Chi or yoga session. It certainly takes longer than a few minutes for you to get the full benefit of the exercise.

The Shapiro's state that "Mindfulness is the awareness of 'something,' while meditation is the awareness of 'nothing.'" (Shapiro & Shapiro, 2017)

Meditation comes in different shapes and forms, whereas mindfulness really only serves the purpose of being able to clear the mind of all the current busyness of the world.

Expanding on the above concepts, here are a couple of other differences between the two.

Meditation is practiced whereas mindfulness improves quality of thought

Mindfulness is reached through focused attention. It is deliberate. It focuses on what is happening right now. Mindfulness passes on judgment on what is happening. You practice meditation though. It is a technique that is used to achieve a specific state within your body and mind.

Meditation develops mindfulness

Through meditation you can become mindful. Mindfulness can be developed through other practices and not just meditation.

There are therapeutic benefits to mindfulness

Many therapists encourage mindful living. This can be achieved without meditation. This is a more popular approach because not all patients are able to practice meditation techniques.

Mindfulness doesn't need a formal process

Instead of having to rely on meditation to achieve a state of mindfulness this can be achieved either in combination with meditation or on its own. Meditation helps the practitioner become aware of what they are experiencing internally. Mindfulness can be used as a means of being intentional. In the moment and fully engaged right now.

Meditation is complex

While mindfulness can be used in many different applications, it does one thing. It allows you to become focused and aware. Meditation on the other hand is way more complex than this. Mindfulness is just one component. It is used to keep the mind from wandering in meditation. Using mindfulness can improve your overall experience of meditation.

Some common characteristics associated with mindfulness, other than simply being present in the moment include:

- Learning how to move beyond things that have happened in the past and leaving them there.
- Connecting to ourselves in a more powerful way. Getting to know who we are right at our core, instead of focusing on things that are superficial.
- Accepting ourselves and others for who we are. The world is full of individuals who feel the need to judge those around them. Not only that but self-judgment prevents us from moving forward. Mindfulness overcomes this.
- With so much happening all around us, we can hold on to mental blocks. We create our own narrative and fear of the future. Instead of being able to live in the moment we live with doubt. Mindfulness can help you see that your focus should be in the present. The past has already happened, there is nothing you can do to prevent the future from happening. The only aspect of your life you really have control over is here and now.

How Meditation & Mindfulness Complement One Another

As you can see these two practices can be quite different from one another. Together however, they complement one another. Many of these points can be applied specifically in the workplace as a means of reducing stress, relieving tension and anxiety, and restoring a sense of peace and calm.

Mindfulness allows you to become more focused on what is happening around you. It can also make you aware of how you might be behaving that needs to change. Mindfulness can also help you feel less stressed. It takes meditation to help you reflect on what has or is taking place.

The two complement each other by allowing your brain to work at a higher level. Laser-like focus can be achieved through mindfulness, which allows you to complete your work, be effective as part of a team, while working toward your goals.

Decision-making without the emotional component means that within business where it is vital to remain objective. This can be achieved through meditation and mindfulness. Combining the two techniques help you step back from the situation, evaluate what is happening without becoming emotionally involved. You can confidently make those decisions without being clouded by unnecessary thoughts and emotions.

Meditation combined with mindfulness can improve creativity. By centering your attention and focus, especially through effective breathing techniques can assist in creative thinking. By shifting focus, you can open your mind to new, exciting ideas that might otherwise not exist because your mind is overfilled with thoughts and emotions based on everything going on around you. By clearing your mind, concentrating on your breathing, being present in the moment, and allowing your brain to connect with those things that are most important.

Rediscover who you really are. Being fully engrossed in work can sometimes make you forget who you really are. A disconnect happens. We may become engaged in what we are doing, but not in who or what we are. We lose focus, we lose passion, we lose satisfaction. The moment you no longer feel passionate about what you are doing the amount of effort spent on the task at hand reduces exponentially.

NOTES

Chapter 2: The Science Behind Meditation & Mindfulness

"Meditation is the only intentional, systematic human activity which at bottom is about not trying to improve yourself to get anywhere else, but simply to realize where you already are."

~ Jon Kabat-Zinn (Kabat-Zinn, 2004)

Since meditation and mindfulness were first introduced to the west it is almost as if rebranded and repackaged into some other form of holistic healing, rather than being promoted as coming from the east. In Chapter 1 I mentioned that when Kabat-Zinn first brought these techniques back to the west, he immediately recognized that for him to be taken seriously there needed to be no mention of its Buddhist roots or the history behind these practices.

Instead, he would include both in his own wellness-based healing under the auspices of sciences and medicine. This chapter will take a closer look at the scientific side of meditation and mindfulness.

Reasons Why Meditation and Mindfulness Improves Your Life

Although each of these practices has been around for centuries and practiced by millions, the scientific aspect of what seems to be simple exercises of the mind and body can result in significant changes to mental health issues.

Like any form of physical exercise, meditation and mindfulness are exactly the same. The more you practice these techniques, the better you become, the greater the overall benefits, and the longer these will last. There's a reason for the comparison to physical exercise. It is not good enough to simply take out gym membership, or visit the gym once in a while, never using any of the equipment. There is no value in having a personal trainer work out a specific fitness regimen for you to follow if you aren't prepared to give it a go, and regularly.

When it comes to similar exercises for the mind and body, it is going to take a whole lot more than just sitting, hoping that your mind will become calm because you have bought a book. You can sit in hope. You can even sit without doing anything… It is still not going to work unless you do something to make it work.

You need to get the process right. There are formal steps that should be followed, things like breathing techniques, focusing the mind and eliminating all other background noise or influences. This is really mindfulness in action. A way to prevent the mind from wandering or being caught up in other things that aren't important.

Meditation allows you to discover what is happening internally. It helps us learn to control how we experience our surroundings, rather than having what's going on around us determine how we respond. We can go through life this way, having one negative experience after the next, purely because we don't know how to change our perception of events.

There is a connection between meditation and the ability to rewire and retrain our brains. This is according to neuroscientists. The result of these changes benefits mental and physical health. The transformation that takes place in the brain is referred to as neuroplasticity. These changes can be both long- and short-term. Neuroplasticity, if you have never heard of it, is defined as being "the ability of the brain to form and reorganize synaptic connections, especially in response to learning or experience or following injury. "Neuroplasticity offers real hope to everyone from stroke victims to dyslexics." (Ackerman,2018)

A study conducted at Harvard University has shown that being able to place the body in a relaxed state, even just for a couple of minutes can interrupt sensations caused by the body responding to inflammation. This shifts toward stabilizing DNA instead. This is not the only short-term advantage. Others include lowering blood pressure, reducing anxiety and stress, and to be honest, who doesn't need that nowadays? There are also benefits when it comes to helping us in our decision-making process. We also learn to focus more and this increases our ability to concentrate on those things that matter most. These are just some of the short-term benefits of meditation. (Bhasin et al., 2013)

Returning to participating in rigorous exercises as part of a fitness routine. In the long run, the health and fitness benefits are numerous. In exactly the same way, habitual meditation practice improves memory functionality in the brain. It helps with emotion regulation and increases compassion and empathy. Through mindfulness we can control our thought process. We begin to leave judgment(s) behind us, making us nicer people to be around. We also become much more resilient. This simply means we find it much easier to bounce back whenever we are faced with any form of failure.

These are just a handful of reasons why our lives can be improved through meditation and mindfulness.

What Illnesses Can it Help With?

The heightened ability to focus so specifically on something can help increase the awareness you have of yourself and your environment. This alone improves concentration.

It can help reduce stress levels, which is a major problem globally. The American Psychological Association conducted a study recently that clearly indicates that stress levels are increasing exponentially. Two polls were conducted recently just months apart. It found that almost 90% of Americans are experiencing some form of stress that is having a major negative impact on their lives. A couple of these common stressors in no particular order, were found to be: (Heckman, 2022)

- Ongoing uncertainty of the Covid-19 pandemic – this is linked to long-term infection, sudden loss of loved ones, infection and debilitating illness.

- Ever increasing unemployment rates.

- Financial stress – money, the economy, cost of living, and inflation. These figures jumped from 59% to 87% within just six months.

- Due to increased stress, many individuals reported they have consumed more alcohol as a coping mechanism. Of course, this only serves to make matters worse as a cycle begins to perpetuate.

- Even things like weight appear close to the top of the list of things Americans are worrying about right now.

- Parents worry about their children. Children in turn worry about the stability of family relationships.

To be honest, this list could continue ad nauseum. I'm sure you get the point though. Stress in all its forms is a contributing factor to declining mental health. Closely associated with stress is both anxiety and depression. Each of these mental health conditions are multi-faceted. What you really need to know is that meditation and mindfulness can have a positive effect on each of these.

Other diseases that can benefit from meditation and mindfulness include:

- Poor concentration ability and an overactive mind. While the two may sound contradictory, Attention-Deficit Hyperactivity Disorder (ADHD) or ADD are two very real problems that don't only affect children. Many adults are trying to cope with these same symptoms.

- Earlier I spoke about pain management and being able to work with inflammation. Being able to calm your minds and redirect your thoughts can help patients battling cancer. While it may not remove the disease, it can certainly place the patient in a positive mental state, making it easier to accept, adapt, or manage the devastating effects of something so life-threatening.

- Trying to recover from addiction – any form of addiction can be really challenging. Whether you are dealing with withdrawal symptoms, cravings, or even trying to maintain the lifestyle you have managed to recreate, these techniques can help you.

- Stress reduction practices can help stabilize blood pressure. There are many diseases that cause high blood pressure. Focused meditation can help regulate this.

- Post-Traumatic Stress Disorder, commonly referred to as PTSD, is more common than you may think. It is not only limited to those serving in war times. What about medical personnel, police, high risk jobs where danger is part of everyday life. Some individuals battle with PTSD as a result of traumatic events in their childhood. It may take years before something triggers it. Meditation can help improve quality of life.

- Meditation can calm the mind to assist with the inability to sleep or experiencing night terrors and sleep disturbances. This is something you can do shortly before retiring, or even in bed. It is a much better option than relying on medication long-term.

- Many might believe that weight control and eating behavior only refers to being overweight, overeating, and binge eating. Sure, each of these can be addressed through meditation, as can eating disorders on the other end of the spectrum – bulimia, anorexia, loss of appetite, sudden weight fluctuations.

Positive State of Mind

These could also be referred to as mental benefits, although many of these are characteristics and personality traits, and even relate to interpersonal skills and how we view ourselves.

- Relating to others and accepting them for who they are
- Self-acceptance, and self-awareness
- Increased tolerance levels
- Attracting peace and calm into your life
- Being able to practice compassion and kindness
- Improved reasoning and cognitive skills
- Dealing with your own emotional intelligence and that of others
- Being more open to change
- Remaining level-headed even in chaos
- Enhanced concentration ability
- Having a clear mental picture
- Reduced worry about the past and future
- Increased mindfulness
- Ability to be fair to self and others
- Greater peace
- Ability to find inner serenity
- Capable of self-control and regulation
- Overall wellness and enhanced wellbeing

Live in the Now and Not in the Past

Having the ability to focus on the present, and this moment is at the heart of meditation and mindfulness. Throughout time, whether practicing Buddhism, Tai Chi, Yoga, or any other form of meditation, most, if not all have a component of centering yourself in the present and focusing on now.

Given the lightning-paced world we are currently living in with all the demands of everyday life as well as daily technological advancements, being able to slow down is challenging. We desperately need to move away from the past, eliminating ruminations of the past and future. For our mental and physical health, we have to find a way to stop and take a breath. To pause, reflect, and make better decisions for the future.

It is humanly impossible for us to keep going at the speed that meets the demands of the world right now without having something to rely on to reset or rewind mentally, physically, and spiritually. By spiritually I refer to that inner peace that you can only really tap into and experience when you are focused on what is happening inside you.

Living in the moment gives you the chance to slow down. To regroup and ground yourself once more. It is becoming aware of everything going on around you right now. To do this you need to be able to quieten your mind, which is what meditation and mindfulness do. Don't worry about what's happening in the background or around you. To tune into present awareness, you need to be able to make use of what is happening internally.

Choosing to accept things for what they are, without becoming all caught up in emotions, especially negative ones can help you move closer to achieving that inner peace. It is more than choosing to do something. It is not necessarily an action, rather than a conscious awareness.

Breathing plays a large part in being able to live in the present. Awareness and gratitude are another two important components.

If you really had to analyze all the emotions attached to past events you could probably make a list that would look something like this:

- Anger with yourself or others.
- Being content and happy. These are memories that may be sugar-coated. You may embellish your memories and experiences as being better than they really were.
- Panic as you recall previous events or experiences.
- Regret for things done or not done.

The future on the other hand is filled with things like,

- Anxiety, stress, and panic.
- Hope for a better future.
- Excitement – this is in anticipation. It may or may not materialize.

Can you see how your thoughts and emotions can become warped and stuck in the past or fixated on the future. In truth, there is nothing you can do about the past because it has already happened. Similarly, you cannot control the future.

You can certainly hope for better things, however, nothing about your future plans for yourself or others is guaranteed.

Living on either side of the present moment can rob ourselves and our loved ones of experiences that we might be enjoying now. When we are fixated on other timelines, we cannot see what is right in front of us. What is happening now that can make us truly happy.

Stages of Meditation

When it comes to meditation the most common form of meditation or process that is relatable to almost anyone would be yoga. I will go through three common stages of yoga meditation and break each down into simplified terminology that is easy to understand and apply.

Terminology may sound a bit strange at first, this is purely because each of the three names are Sanskrit, or a language that was common to ancient Hindu (Indian).

These three stages are to help us become focused and centered. To look at how we see ourselves internally and externally, and finally to combine our focus to change our state of being.

If you can imagine a pendulum swinging between two points from side to side, this is very much how our mind works. We are constantly in a state of flux between being able to concentrate fully on something, and having our focus drawn in the opposite direction by distractions. As long as it keeps on swinging we have no control over where our mind goes or what we think.

There are two realities constantly presenting themselves. What is happening around us, and what is happening inside us. An external reality, and internal reality. Irrespective, each of these realities are subjected to our own perceptions. We don't necessarily see them as they really are. We see them through filters, through lenses of our own creation. We interpret each of these through our belief system. Through values we may have been taught, through experiences, and memories.

External realities are processed through our senses. They are based on what we can physically experience. Because it is external it is usually something tangible. Something you can actually touch or feel. Something tactile. It is concentrating on something visual, audible, and even sensory in terms of smell. Whatever it is we still surround the external reality with our own association of the item. What does it make us feel, what do we remember about it, does it evoke a memory, an emotion?

The second of these realities is what we feel internally. This concept is simple enough to understand. What's happening inside ourselves. It is being aware of sensations happening internally. Things like our heartbeat, breathing, and being able to focus our thoughts. Internal realities are all processed mentally. There will always be perceptions attached to this type of thinking.

At the beginning stages of learning meditation techniques, you can make use of either internal or external realities. This process is used for training our minds to focus on one thing at a time until we can do this automatically.

Stage one

Referred to as Dharana. In Sanskrit this means being able to concentrate. To focus your attention on something without being distracted. Whether this is something tangible like the sound of water flowing over rocks, or the flickering light of a candle. Being able to engage the mind fully is the key to achieving this stage. Some find it easier to pay close attention to their breathing as they inhale and exhale. To the rise and fall of their chest.

Stage two

Is called Dhyana, another Sanskrit word that means "reflect." This is where focus moves to concentration. It describes the ability to meditate. Definitions of Sanskrit are quite similar, yet still diverse. It refers to the mind, moving, or being able to think. To successfully achieve this point, you should have control over your posture, your breathing, and your concentration.

Stage three

Also known as Samadhi. By the time you reach this stage you have reached the highest place you can be. In Sanskrit, it translates to "together," "toward," "bliss," and "enlightenment." You can see how combining each of these words together can give you a clear picture of this final stage. It symbolizes your connection with something higher than yourself. Some refer to this as the divine, connecting with deity, or becoming fully enlightened. It is also seen as being able to achieve a spiritual connection.

NOTES

Chapter 3: The Motivation Behind Meditation & Mindfulness

> *"To make the right choices in life, you have to get in touch with your soul. To do this, you need to experience solitude, which most people are afraid of, because in the silence you hear the truth and know the solutions."*
>
> ~ Deepak Chopra (The Editors at Chopra.com, 2018)

Like most things in life, we should choose to do things intentionally. This means doing things with a reason, with some form of motivation behind it. When it comes to meditation these reasons could be varied and diverse. You might even say that your reasons are as unique as you are. There are a number of reasons that are fairly common and they are central to why we choose to meditate. Let's take a closer look at what some of these motivations might be.

In Chapter 7 I will include a number of guided meditations that will assist you as you work through some very specific life situations. Before we can get there however, we should consider what drives us toward meditation.

Motivations to Meditate

A couple of these reasons or motivations include:

Relationships

It doesn't matter if we are trying to strengthen a current relationship with a family member, a loved one, a work colleague, an employer, employee, customer, and even with strangers. We can meditate on areas of any of these relationships that may need attention. Perhaps we are battling to connect and communicate effectively. Maybe there is a situation that needs to be resolved, a wound that needs healing.

By focusing your intention through meditation, you may find the clarity you need to find the answers you seek. Many individuals use meditation to develop a much closer relationship with deity, with a higher power, with the universe, or other life force. This will differ from person to person and is something that is very personal. Whether used as a tool for spirituality or enlightenment, being able to tap into the source. Relationships on a variety of levels is often a driving force behind quiet reflection.

Environments

Seeking answers and ways to deal with different environments we find ourselves in on this journey we call life can be a valid reason to meditate. It doesn't matter whether you are looking for answers to a work dilemma, ways to connect with your family in the home, even if this is searching for peace and harmony in the midst of what could only be described as chaos. Perhaps meditation could help you prepare for school assignments, college exams, business presentations, or simply coming to terms with things going on around us daily.

Situations

We all find ourselves in different situations we have to face. Being able to meditate can help us work through each of these in a more calm, rational way. Naturally we can't be prepared for every situation that life might throw in our direction. Some of these situations might be life changing. Moving house, relocating to a new state or even something as drastic as moving half-way around the world.

These things are stressful. You can become grounded and centered, making these transitions easier. What about searching for employment? Changing relationships or relationship status. Marriage, divorce, even moving in together. Anything that shifts and changes from what you are used to, to something unknown can be unsettling. What lies ahead is uncertain. One of the ways to reduce emotional stress is through meditation.

These are a few simple examples of different situations; I am sure you can think of many others. Maybe you are facing some things right now that you need to devote some quiet time to. This is what meditation is all about.

Health

This is a huge reason to meditate. There will come a time in each of our lives when we are faced with health challenges. Perhaps the health challenges aren't even our own. You never know when a serious health issue is going to arise. Whether it is as a result of an accident or something that's hereditary. The one thing about health is that it is unpredictable. Meditation has long been used for all forms of health benefits. From pain management, to dealing with debilitating mental health problems such as chronic illness, anxiety, stress, and depression.

Death

The unexpected, or even anticipated loss of a loved one is always going to be cause for major emotional upheaval in your life. No matter how you are connected, whether friend, spouse, loved one, parent or child. Death symbolizes the end. The end of a journey. Feelings of helplessness or hopelessness could follow. Being able to meditate can open your heart and mind to peace and understanding, rather than being filled with loss, mourning, and even anger. Meditation can bring us to a point of acceptance.

Faith

While I have mentioned that meditation is often used to connect with that higher power that we recognize spiritually, it can also be used to strengthen our faith. When we find we have questions that we are battling to find answers to. Meditation can help us find answers using a rational mind rather than a frantic one.

Other areas of our lives that are a sound motivation for us to meditate are for things like, healing, dealing with trauma, love, empathy, compassion, and success.

Reasons for meditation

Take out the trash

Get rid of all the negative thoughts, energy, and emotions you drag around with you all the time. This can often accumulate pretty quickly. Meditation helps relieve you of a lot of this negative energy that drains you and keeps you from living your best life. Think of meditation as a way of being able to empty a trash can that's constantly being filled with things that aren't necessary. We are exposed to these things each day. What we choose to do with these things can ultimately determine our happiness and our path toward progression.

What are you thinking

We constantly have thoughts racing through our minds. Regardless of whether we want them or not. Most of these thoughts are subconscious. Have you ever tried to focus on one thing and without even realizing it all of a sudden your mind has taken you somewhere completely off track? The problem is that we can't be in control of our thoughts every second of each day. We can however become more self-aware through meditation. It can help you clear a lot of what you don't want to be thinking about and slow down thinking. Quieten your mind. It can help you figure out what is really important and where you should be placing your focus.

Consciousness and calm

Is your reality running away from you or can you bring your mind sharply into focus so you know what you need to do. Can you tap into your inner consciousness and become grounded or do you feel as though the world is swallowing you up? You can slow things down to the point where you can look at things objectively, being able to think rationally before you act.

Sleep and insomnia

Adding meditation techniques to your evening routine can help even those who have battled with insomnia most of their lives. Research has shown that within just eight weeks chronic sufferers were enjoying quality sleep for longer periods at nighttime. (Ong et al., 2014)

Less stress

Meditation has been used by business executives in some of the most stressful positions including Silicon Valley, and Wall Street has been using meditation to reduce stress for years. Harvard Medical School completed a study in 2005 that proved that meditation could actually change the physical structure of the brain. (Lazar et al., 2005)

Binge eating

Mindful eating was taught to a group of women as part of a research study conducted by the University of San Francisco. Meditation formed a large part of this process. Results for the group taught to meditate reduced stress, and abdominal fat. (Daubenmier et al., 2011)

Faster healing through pain reduction

In the 1980s Jon Kabat-Zinn first introduced that meditation could be used as a means of pain relief. (Zeidan et al., 2012)

The program he developed in the 1980s, Mindfulness-Based Stress Reduction is still successful today.

Worry and anxiety

Thanks to the challenges of modern-day life it has become normal for us to catastrophize events. We focus on all the bad, anticipating the worst at any given moment. Of course, all those things we worry about seldom occur. This doesn't mean that our lives become less stressful. Anxiety is something that is very real. Learning to meditate can greatly reduce the effects of this type of stress that we place on ourselves.

Self-awareness

Meditation can help us see through all the negativities we insist on carrying around with us. It can help us sift through our emotions, being able to tell which are real and which are just as a result of negative thinking. Focusing on negativity robs us of our happiness. You have the power to determine where your thoughts go.

Relaxation

We all know what it feels like to become tightly wound up because of traffic, waiting for results, anticipating a life-changing event… Learning to relax both mind and body can reduce stress throughout the body. We are wired to deal with stress from the day we are born. It is instinctive of self-preservation and while this is more commonly referred to as the "fight or flight" response, our bodies go through a chemical change when this instinct is triggered. Being able to relax through meditation can negate this response.

All you need is love

Meditation can really help you get in touch with your emotions. As you do you can communicate these better with your significant other. Studies found that those who knew how to meditate were able to express their emotions more openly and interpersonal relationships were improved. (Wanderlust, 2018)

Understanding Mindfulness

According to the Merriam-Webster dictionary there are two distinct definitions of mindfulness. The first is "the quality or state of being mindful." While the second is "the practice of maintaining a nonjudgmental state of heightened or complete awareness of one's thoughts, emotions, or experiences on a moment-to-moment basis." (Merriam-Webster Dictionary, 2019)

Living in the modern day and age that is so fast-paced it is understandable that things often feel completely out of control. We feel like we are on an ever-spinning hamster wheel, unable to slow down or get off. The thing about mindfulness is being able to slow that wheel down, at least to the point where you can once again tune into your own thoughts and emotions. This is without adopting the thoughts and emotions of those around you. Instead, it is being able to apply the thoughts and emotions you have within yourself.

Mindfulness can not only provide you with a sense of peace, but there are ways you can use it to your advantage to strengthen the relationship you have with others. It is misleading to believe that mindfulness and meditation are the same thing. Sure, they can be used individually, or in conjunction with one another, however, mindfulness can be used at any time. Meditation on the other hand takes a certain amount of planning, an allocation of a reasonable amount of time, and moving through several different stages for it to be effective.

Mindfulness is bringing yourself to a point of awareness. It allows you to genuinely reflect on yourself, your emotions, your thoughts, your actions, and everything else you happen to be going through at the time.

Jon Kabat-Zinn describes mindfulness this way, "The awareness that arises from paying attention, on purpose, in the present moment and non-judgmentally" (Booth, 2017). Because he is one of the fathers of mindfulness, this definition is widely accepted as being closest to describing what mindfulness is.

If we break down what he is saying, he describes how we should direct our consciousness to the moment. Not a collection of time, like an hour, or for the next week. Instead, it is a moment-by-moment activity. The present moment refers to what is happening here and now, rather than what is taking place around you. Mindfulness forms part of meditation, however, you can practice mindfulness without having to meditate.

We have a very specific need for mindfulness today as a result of the way our daily activities have changed. Today we are far more reliant on social media. We crave the attention from those we know and even strangers. We thrive off of "likes" and "retweets." We desperately feel we need the approval of others. In truth, this is most of what is driving us insane. These are the things that keep us up at night. The thoughts that are all consuming, rather than focusing our energy in the present.

Getting into the nuts and bolts of what mindfulness is, exactly the same as meditation, it has existed for many centuries. This is not something that is new age mumbo-jumbo that has been introduced to deal with modern issues by modern scientists, therapists, or other practitioners working with various coping strategies. Mindfulness can be traced back to Buddha. His theory of mindfulness was another simple one – that the mind is a powerful force. One where we can create our own sense of reality. It is allowing the mind to determine how we feel about ourselves. Whether we are happy or experiencing immense sorrow. We attract our own misery or happiness into our lives. We are really the ones responsible for how we see and feel about ourselves.

You might view this self-assessment or analysis as being able to reflect or look at ourselves. What we need to learn from doing this in a mindful way is keeping judgment out of it. This is much easier said than done because we are and have been raised in an environment that is filled with competitiveness. As part of this competitive streak, we feel the need to compare ourselves to those around us. We compare ourselves physically. We compare our accomplishments, our financial status, our achievements, homes, families, and anything else that might seem like it is important. We want to be better than the next person. In reality, each of these things simply drain us. They shift our focus from the present. Concentrate on the past… What we have achieved, what we have managed to accumulate, the amount of money and wealth we have been able to acquire.

We focus on the future. Where are we going? How can we be better than the next person? What is it going to take to have that position of power over those in our social circle? The problem with focusing on the past and the future is that we miss the present. We don't recognize what we are doing right now. We are out of touch with our emotions, our thoughts, our self-awareness, and how we act and react to those things happening all around us.

Mindfulness lets us strengthen the muscles of our minds, making them malleable. As we train ourselves to get rid of all forms of judgment, we begin to be kinder, and more understanding as we begin to view ourselves and our thoughts differently. Mindfulness can help us relax both body and mind.

Because we are focused on the present, our thoughts are reduced. We minimize the thoughts of the past, and the thoughts of the future, simply allowing anything that is not really necessary to disappear into the background. Although we are present it is also as though we are watching in from a distance. We can focus on each of the things that are most important, for this very moment.

Something worth mentioning is that our thoughts wander. This is quite normal and will happen time and time again. When this happens, acknowledge your thoughts, and return to your meditation practice. It will take time but eventually your mind will develop the skill to ignore them. Figure out what works best for you. Perhaps this is by focusing your mind on a body scan, concentrating on your breathing, or something else. Just know that you will be able to control your thoughts as you work on mindfulness.

Now that you have a better insight into your reasons for meditation, and what mindfulness is all about, it is time to move onto putting some of these things into practice. You don't need to be an expert in understanding everything about mindfulness and meditation in order to begin to apply it to your life. All you need is a willingness to try.

NOTES

Chapter 4: Learning the Art of Practice

"Breathing in, I calm my body and mind. Breathing out, I smile. Dwelling in the present moment I know this is the only moment."

~ Thich Nhat Hanh (Nhât Hạnh, Thích, 2008)

It's all fine learning about all these interesting facts and information about meditation and mindfulness. What's even more important is being able to put these things into practice. It is really only through practice that we get to not only discover more about ourselves but we learn something new each day. We can begin to push ourselves further. Open our minds and hearts more and discover the inner peace that is there waiting for us.

New beginnings can be scary. Fear is one of the greatest obstacles in our way. We may feel inspired to give this form of quiet introspection a go. Don't expect to be perfect at it from the outset. That is simply unrealistic. Find that starting point and move forward from there at your own pace. Even if you have decided to do this with a friend or as part of a group—don't measure your own level of competence with someone else. Just as we are each individual we are each unique with our own set of strengths and limitations. You may find it is easier for you to breathe than it is for you to keep your mind from wandering.

What is Practice and Why you should

Just as anything else in life, if you really want to become good at it, or learn to master these techniques, you will need to practice. When I refer to practice this doesn't mean doing it once or twice and expecting to move onto the next level. For many it will take months and even years of disciplined practice to get the technique under your belt.

One of the greatest gifts that learning how to meditate correctly can give you is that you do not need to be a specific age, you don't need any special qualifications to meditate. You don't even need to go to a yoga studio to get it right. Able bodied, disabled, young, old, there are no limitations or requirements necessary.

To describe exactly what it is, is maybe learning how to recognize your thoughts and emotions for what they are. Name them. Recognize them and where they come from. Then, understand and accept that you are not these thoughts. You are not these emotions. You are you!

Meditation doesn't need to be a long-drawn-out thing. You can spend as little as 5-minutes a day, to more than 30-minutes. The secret to its efficacy is consistency and this is where it becomes hard. Even the most seasoned, experienced meditator will tell you that they battle to keep their focus under control for this length of time. Perhaps that is the reason why meditative exercises such as yoga and Thai Chi are easier. Because you are actively doing something rather than simply clearing your mind of everything and keeping it that way for any extent of time. It doesn't really matter, there's no where that states you should stick to this length of time or that length of time. It is believed, however, that spending as little as 10-minutes each day can have a marked influence on both your health and happiness.

The difficulty comes in being able to sit (lotus pose or not) where your brain is completely devoid of any thoughts whatsoever. It is impossible. Those rambling, never-ending, mind-numbing thoughts that occupy every part of the brain are all-consuming. Even when you are trying to think of nothing. Maybe especially when you are trying to think of nothing whatsoever. Try it for a minute. Close your eyes and try to think of nothing at all! Guaranteed you can't do it.

You will begin to think about some of the most arbitrary things. That constant stream of thoughts that cross the stage of your mind never seem to come to an end. Even when you are doing your best to ignore them. You tell yourself that they are unimportant and try to shove them out the way. They just keep coming.

Things as random as wondering whether dinner is being prepared or what to make for dinner, should you apply for that promotion, or are you convinced that Dave from accounting is going to get it? You wonder whether the outfit you selected for your child's performance is good enough. Maybe you should stop and look for something else? The increase in the fuel price is going to mean that maybe you can't take that vacation at the end of the year. The kids are going to be so disappointed. You haven't spoken to your folks for a while. It really should have been a priority, but with so much going on with the tight deadlines you have to meet, time just seems to run away with you. Tomorrow. What's on Netflix that's good? And they just keep coming. Can you see how it is easy to go through between 45,000 and 60,000 thoughts every single day?

If ever there has been a desperate need for us to be able to quieten our thoughts, clear our minds of all the garbage and learn to focus on serenity, it is now. But how? Where do you even begin?

Meditation has the capacity to help us cut back on those thoughts we don't really need. It's like being able to skip through those thoughts that are literally just background noise, keeping only those that are important. Some of the immediate benefits of being able to do this is to become more conscious of what we are thinking. Imagine for a moment that your mind is completely out of focus because of all the junk that's there. You are looking for something you need to be able to move the clutter around. You really need to be able to focus. Perhaps even sharpening your focus to get rid of the stuff that's unnecessary.

The brain is possibly one of the most important muscles in the body. Without it we don't have the capacity to control any part of our lives. When this is exercised regularly and strengthened then all other areas of our lives can also benefit. Divide your life up into areas that make up who you are. There are at least eight areas that are most common when looking at the different aspects of what we are all about:

- Spirituality
- Relationships
- Emotional health
- Employment
- Learning
- Well-being

- Physical health
- Finances

As you focus on each of these areas you can begin to cut through all the drama and unnecessary noise that you don't need in your life.

Let's take a closer look at getting started and where to even begin.

Body scan

If you want to know where to begin with meditation it may be worthwhile knowing what's going on internally. Where do you need to focus your attention? This is easier than you may think. It will give you that starting point. You will begin by completing a simple body scan. What are the benefits to giving this a go?

- It can help with insomnia and other sleep related problems
- Focused pain management
- Relieves stress, anxiety, and depression
- Self-awareness, understanding, and compassion
- Can assist with addictive behavior

Getting started

1. The easiest way to get started with this is by lying in a relaxed position where you have room around your body for you to be able to stretch and flex your muscles.

2. Inhale and exhale deeply. Pay close attention to each breath as you fill your lungs to capacity and exhale. Can you feel the oxygen?

3. Choose an area of the body that you would like to begin scanning. This doesn't matter whether you want to begin at the tips of your toes or the top of your head.

4. Spend time focusing just on that area. Continue breathing. What does the area feel like? What can you feel? Are your muscles in that area aching? Is there tingling happening? Pay close attention, especially when something feels out of the ordinary.

5. Don't rush this process. Take as long as you need. Move across your entire body following the same process. You are going to use mindfulness as you come across any sensation, pain, muscle stiffness, ache, or anything else that seems to be different. Notice it, recognize it, acknowledge it, accept it, and move on. Recognize your emotions for what they are as you go through this process. If you are hurting, take note of this but let it go. Don't judge yourself.

6. Imagine the pain decreasing as you continue breathing. If there is tension, imagine this becoming less. Breathe in the calm, breathe out the pain!

7. Move on to the next part of your body. Pay close attention to each area. Focus on your muscles, bones, internal organs. How do they feel? Is there tension? Is

there pain? What can you tell as you move through this whole process slowly?

8. Be intentional in your focus. You may discover that those unwanted thoughts that are totally unrelated to what you are doing begin wandering back into your head. Recognize them and dismiss them. Gently pull your focus back and continue scanning your body.

9. Take as long as you need as you move right across each section of your body individually. Once you have done this, re-scan your body as a whole. Imagine you are taking x-rays. You have managed to complete each area of your body, now it is time to get a better picture of your entire body. Begin at one end, ending at the other. All the while you are completing this process, you are inhaling and exhaling, concentrating on your breathing.

10. Once you have completed this entire process you can slowly return to the present. There's a strong possibility that you will now have a better idea of areas of your body that need work.

A body scan can often sort out whatever is wrong. Other times you may find that physical pain or discomfort will suddenly be triggered. What often happens is that because of this you may feel that meditation isn't worth it. All it's doing is making you feel even worse. This is where many individuals make a mistake. They throw the towel in too soon. Before they have even given themselves a chance to begin to make a difference. Keep at it. Whatever you do, don't give up just yet.

Breathing exercises

There are many different breathing exercises out there that can be used for different applications, from reducing stress, addressing anxiety, increasing your lung capacity, reducing your heart rate, and simply to relax. These are just some of the ways breathing can improve your life. Of course, there are many other benefits, as you improve your oxygen intake, you will be able to see the results for yourself. When you first begin to add breathing exercises into your day, you may need to start off small. For breathing exercises to be effective you need to make use of them regularly. Start off small at the beginning until you are comfortable with the technique you find that works best for you.

I'm going to go through some of these different breathing exercises along with the guided meditation processes in Chapter 7 but in the meantime I will briefly mention some of the different types of breathing styles. The one that works best for me personally is what is known as diaphragmatic breathing or belly breathing. I will use this as an example. Because this works for me doesn't mean that it is going to be the most effective breathing technique for you. It's worth giving a couple a try over a period of time to see where you get the greatest benefit.

Let's take a closer look at belly breathing and how to practice it till it becomes second nature. This form of breathing actually teaches you to breathe properly by filling your lungs to capacity. When you first start out, spend about five to ten minutes a day doing the exercise below.

Belly breathing

Here's how:

Find somewhere that you won't be disturbed for the duration of this breathing exercise. It needs to be somewhere comfortable.

1. Lie on your back with your knees slightly bent. Be sure to be comfortable. You may want to place a pillow just under your knees to support your legs slightly. Rest your head on a pillow as well.

2. One of your hands should be placed on your stomach just below your ribs with the other on your chest, across your breastbone area.

3. Breathe in through your nose slowly. You should feel your stomach rise against your hand.

4. The hand across your upper chest should be kept still.

5. Breathe out through your mouth with your lips in a blowing position. While you are doing this, your stomach muscles should be tightened as you breathe out slowly. At the same time the other hand across the top of your chest should remain in the same place.

Keep repeating each of these steps for the amount of time you have chosen. Be sure to try and do this exercise three to four times a day.

Equal breathing

Here, both inhaling and exhaling are done to exactly the same count. If you inhale over a count of three, you should exhale using the same count of three. The benefit of this type of breathing is restoring balance.

Focused breathing

By choosing a word or set of words you can use your imagination during these exercises. This type of breathing helps with stress relief. You can improve your focus as the name suggests. There's no difference in your breathing, you simply focus on it intently. While breathing in you might be visualizing breathing in light and peace, and while exhaling, breathing out stress and anger. Whatever your focus it can help relieve you of negative thinking.

Nostril breathing

Breathing through each nostril on its own can improve your heart rate. They say this is best for being able to relax. The key to this type of breathing is being able to breathe through each nostril without feeling blocked or congested. Don't try this if you are battling with sinus or a head cold! This is relatively simple. You breathe in through one nostril and out through the alternate nostril. Alternate by breathing in through the same nostril you just exhaled through and breathing out through the other nostril. Repeat this process several times.

Pursed lip

Benefits of this type of breathing is to help regulate breathing, especially when battling with shortness of breath. It increases your oxygen intake while helping you get rid of carbon dioxide. The point is to release any stale air remaining in your lungs. Many physical illnesses cause shortness of breath. This exercise can help with these symptoms.

These are just a couple of breathing techniques that are fairly common. There are loads more which we will include in the final chapter.

Relaxation

This may seem like something strange to have to practice but the truth is that very few of us actually know how to relax properly. A lot of this stems from our current lifestyle. Everything around us is busy and even when you think you are going to sit back and "relax" for the evening, or you make plans to take a weekend off, we don't really relax at all.

Thanks to that built-in "fight-or-flight" response that is inherent in all of us is thanks to our ancestors. Way back in history when they were hunter-gatherers, this instinct would warn them when danger was approaching. It was a means of preservation. While this may still be the case today, coming down from one of these fight-or-flight reactions to a situation can take some time. All the while, stress hormones set the body into a tailspin. Your heart is racing, palms are sweating, your breathing changes. Unless you can get your body to return to normal it could become a long-term thing. Ways to move out of this space include deep breathing exercises, yoga, meditation, finding some way to become grounded again or re-focused. Some people find spending time in nature useful while others may choose to have a massage.

A combination between several of the techniques we're discussing in this chapter can help with relaxation. Meditation is believed to work best. It's really worthwhile recognizing that many of the things we believe are a way for us to relax actually aren't. The moment you find your mind wandering down those worrisome paths, you should know that your mind is still full of all the concerns that are making you anxious and stressed to begin with.

Visualization

So, you may be wondering what visualization has to do with meditation and mindfulness. Being able to see things in a positive light can help you overcome negative thinking. It can even help prepare you to face things that you may be afraid of.

Visualization is nothing new. It has just become more popular over the years as people have learned to apply it to sports, work, goal setting and achievement, to gaining self-confidence, and more.

A couple of benefits of being able to see things clearly with your mind's eye, using your imagination to see things mentally in pictures, include:

- Being healthier
- Better performance
- Dealing with depression
- Greater confidence
- Improved sleep
- Laser-like focus
- Less stress
- Reduced anxiety
- Reducing chronic pain

There is a difference between normal visualization and meditation using visualization. There are some similarities, but they are not the same thing. Here's how they differ:

- Meditation relaxes you while visualization fires up the creative part of the brain.
- Visualization can be used to rewire your nervous system, meditation on the other hand calms it down.
- You meditate clearing your mind of thoughts and distractions. Visualization on the other hand needs you to be reactive and aware of what's happening around you.

The best time of day

One of the most common questions most individuals ask when first starting to meditate is what time of day is best to meditate. This is really something personal to you. It depends on your routine and the type of meditation you are planning on doing.

Most people find it beneficial to meditate first thing in the morning. They have felt the benefits of being able to start their day in a stress-free and focused state. For others, the evening is better—at the end of a particularly busy or stressful day. Meditation can help them relax, unwind, regroup their thoughts and prepare themselves for better sleep.

There's no right or wrong answer when it comes to finding the best time of day to meditate. What's more important is actually doing it. Making it a habit and having it become part of your daily routine. When putting this into practice there are a couple of things to keep in mind:

- Stick with the same routine. If you decide you are going to meditate in the morning then stick with it at this time of the day.

- Find a place to meditate that is right for you. The ideal is somewhere calm and inviting. Ventilation should be good so that you are comfortable. No distractions. This is possibly the key to successful meditation. You need to be able to do it without being interrupted.

- Set a goal that you will stick with so it becomes a habit and forms part of your daily routine. One of the ways that people form habits is by tying them to some behavior you are already doing each day. Maybe immediately before you shower. You are already showering each morning. It is automatic. Tie your meditation activity to this. Set your intention to "meditate for 10-minutes before showering each morning."

Start small

As you begin meditating you should start off small. Don't set unrealistic goals. Before trying to get into the habit of meditating properly, give yourself a chance to get into the right frame of mind. Here are a couple of ways you can do this:

- As with any goal you need to find a starting point no matter how small. Before you even think about meditating it may be worthwhile learning how to calm your mind for a short period of time first. You may want to begin with just a couple of minutes where you sit doing nothing, trying to clear your mind of all the noise. This might sound overly simplified yet as you begin to do it you will discover that it's more difficult than you could initially imagine.

- You can begin to build on this slowly until you can sit quietly for longer. Once you can do this you are possibly ready to begin meditating.

- Some other things you should maybe think of as you begin to start off small is getting your timing right. Choose what time of the day works best for you and settle on that. Guided meditations are also a good way to start, having that vocal guidance at regular intervals helps you to refocus the mind if it has wandered without you realizing. Some meditation Apps mentioned in the Resources section will be a good starting point.

- Stop stressing about what you need to do. A lot of people when starting out are more worried about whether they should be lying down, sitting up, using a yoga mat, playing gentle music in the background, having candles burning—and so on! Can you see how tiring and distracting this might be? Don't worry about any of this stuff. All you need is somewhere that works for you where you won't be interrupted.

Basic techniques

Meditation basics broken down as simply as possible look something like this:

- Find a comfortable position. By now you should already know whether you are more comfortable sitting, lying down, crossing your legs, or being in your comfortable chair.

- Begin by taking a couple of deep breaths, inhale and exhale, whilst taking in your surroundings. The sound you make as you exhale should be loud enough for someone to hear if they were in the same room as you. As you begin to relax, close your eyes.

- We've covered a couple of breathing techniques above. When you first begin, don't worry about your breathing. Your breathing can now return to its normal pace, deep breathing only needs to be at the initial stage, prior to closing your eyes.

- Pay attention to each breath though. How does it feel as you inhale and exhale? Don't change your breathing at all during this time.

Start off small as indicated above. Stick with this for a couple of minutes a day. Expand this time as you are feeling comfortable doing so. Once you have managed to master this you have successfully completed the very basics of meditation.

Intermediate techniques

By now you can focus your mind for an extended period of time. You feel that you are now ready to get into the nuts and bolts of meditating properly. Some of these include the following:

Being in the moment

Awareness means being able to tune out things that are distracting. These could be internal like our thoughts, how we feel, our emotional state. To deal with these internal distractions we should give ourselves a set amount of time where we simply focus on clearing our minds of anything and everything that's taking up our focus. We do this by setting an intention to let these things go.

Bringing mindfulness into what you are doing you, release any judgment or other ideas you may have about yourself, your situation, or others. Shift your focus to the here and now. Anything other than this is not important. We need to be present in the moment.

Calm your inner voice

Get rid of that nagging voice that seems to drone on and on about things that aren't important. Usually, the dialogue is all negative and tries to distract us by filling our head with everything that's wrong. It's time you ignore those voices that try to convince you that you're at fault and the reason why your life has turned out the way it has.

The only way to deal with this inner voice is by being aware of what it's telling you. To get this right we have to pay attention to what's passing through our mind at every given moment. Having to deal with a never-ending supply of thoughts can be overwhelming. Being able to work through your inner voice is not something that's easy, or something you'll succeed at immediately. It is going to take practice and effort. By paying close attention to each thought we get to recognize when there's a pause between thinking. Applying mindfulness techniques, we can acknowledge the thought and simply let it go without allowing it to sabotage you.

Improve your focus

You can only improve your focus as you cut back on all the distractions and noise. It is having the ability to concentrate on just one thing. As you begin meditating you focus on your breathing. Now, you might want to focus on something other than breathing. An object of some description is recommended. This might be something in the distance that you focus on. Perhaps it is an expression, mantra, or affirmation. When you are mindful and in the moment by focusing on one single thing it becomes easier to minimize and eliminate other distractions.

The key ingredient for meditation is that this focus is positive. Concentrate on those things that are calming, peaceful, and relaxing. The objective is to release as much stress and anxiety as possible.

Transformation

Meditation is more than simply just sitting and breathing, focusing on what your chest is doing. It is being able to take control of all those moments. Recognizing when moments appear. The purpose of meditation is to become better. To clear our thoughts and emotions from negativity and replace these with positive energy. It has a lot to do with what we think about. Realizing that you can let go of those things that aren't working for you is empowering. What is even more powerful is coming to terms with the fact that you can actually reprogram your thinking—shifting the negative. Focusing on the positive instead. It is being able to change our habits. Out with the old and in with the new.

We often hold onto destructive habits purely because they are that—a habit. That's not to say that because we've had them so long that they are right for us. Meditation can give us the tools we need to be able to take that long look at ourselves, from a point of no judgment, but from the view of being honest. What is it that we are thinking? What do we believe? How are these thoughts and beliefs impacting our actions and the trajectory of our lives?

A lot of the way we live is based on perceptions. The perception we have of the world, or those around us, and even our role in the world. What we think and believe doesn't make it right. Becoming acutely aware of each of these things is exactly what will give us the tools to be able to change. To transform from where we are now, to where we need to be.

Become committed

The more you practice meditating and being mindful at the same time, the easier you will find being able to focus with minimum distractions. You will have greater control over your mind and your thoughts. Where you battled with focus before because there was too much going on inside your head, you will now be able to be present and in the moment. You can now direct your thoughts to where you want them to be, rather than letting them dictate to you where they go.

As you can control your thoughts you can control your mood, and your actions. You can choose to be calm, and happy, rather than stressed out, worried, or overwhelmed. What's happening around you has far less influence over you. You can control your emotions better and choose to be happy.

Advanced techniques

By now you know the basics of being able to relax, focus on your breathing or on a specific object to clear your mind. You are prepared for that barrage of thoughts that keep invading your mind and have learned to guide a wandering mind back toward refocusing for meditation.

You can begin to deepen your meditation with at least an hour that's free of technology. By now you've identified the best time of the day for you to meditate. Here are a couple of things you can add to your current routine:

- Begin and end your meditation session with some yoga, stretches, listening to calming music, chanting, or singing.

- In Hindu there are specific chants that are used however you can choose anything that is going to help focus your thoughts. These chants are directed at Hindu deities done in reverence.

- With many different faiths you can choose something that resonates with you. It can be a mantra, an affirmation, a hymn. The reason why music is effective is it takes concentration which in turn allows you to focus your thoughts in one direction.

- You don't need to chant or sing throughout your meditation session; it should just be there to help ease you into being able to meditate.

- Find a short phrase you can repeat.

- At the end of your meditation session, you may want to stretch slowly while you return to the present. Irrespective of how your meditation experience has been for the day, be grateful and happy. Look at things positively.

Some people will do another brief session of yoga to help increase energy levels.

Accept that it may take time

Be patient with yourself as you begin this journey into meditation. It is going to take time for you to get used to being still both internally and externally. If you can only manage five minutes at a time then that's at least a starting point.

There's no set time frame when it comes to moving through the different techniques of meditation. Some people have been meditating for 20 or so years and still go through bad days. Be patient with yourself and most importantly take things at your own pace.

Don't feel bad if you get bored or fall asleep

Deep meditation can easily lead to you feeling tired or falling asleep completely. Don't be hard on yourself. It happens. By sitting upright without a support behind your back if possible you can be reminded that you are meditating.

Falling asleep may be an outer manifestation of inner exhaustion or it could also be that your body is so relaxed that you are comfortable and content. It can take a while to find the perfect balance between mindful meditation and being alert.

Some other ways to minimize this could include:

- The area should be well lit.
- Change your meditation time.
- Be sure there is enough oxygen and air flowing through the room.
- Find a focal point that you can concentrate on.
- Join a group instead of meditating on your own.
- Meditate before eating rather than trying to do it when you are full.
- Take a break. Stretch, walk around, drink water. Whatever you do, be mindful of your actions.
- Use guided meditations. These can help you stay focused through the whole meditation process.

Having gone through loads of ways you can practice meditating, the key here is to "practice." It doesn't help attempting this once or twice and because you can't get it right the first time, you abandon all hope. There is way more to it than just wanting or wishing for it to happen. You have to be prepared to give it a solid chance. Not only to develop a habit, but also to get the greatest benefit out of it.

NOTES

Chapter 5: How Meditation & Mindfulness Benefit Us All

"Meditation is the only intentional, systematic human activity which at the bottom is about not trying to improve yourself or get anywhere else, but simply to realize where you already are."

~ Jon Kabat-Zinn (Juma, 2022)

Practicing meditation and mindfulness is a lifelong pursuit. Even the most experienced yogis and meditators will tell you that not every meditation session is a great one. You may be thinking to yourself that surely that's the point of being able to meditate? To improve the experience each time you do it. Make no mistake, it will improve, and yes, you will begin to feel the benefits in your life almost immediately. But be realistic in your expectations. Not everything runs perfectly every time.

This chapter will take a closer look at some of the benefits we can experience in our own lives, but also how meditation and mindfulness can benefit those around us. You'd be amazed by how far reaching these benefits are.

Us and them

Meditation not only benefits us but also those who are important to us. The list of benefits is long and detailed, I am going to mention just a few of these – I am sure you will get the main idea as you work through this list. There will probably be others you have seen in your own life and the lives of those around you. Take some time out and include this in the "NOTES" section.

Awareness is increased. Not only awareness of what is taking place within you and all around you, but awareness of how loved ones and those you are close to may be experiencing. Your focus shifts from you to the relationship you have with others.

As your awareness increases, you begin paying more attention. Not just to your surroundings but attention to what is important to you in the moment—this moment.

Your brain begins to function on a higher level. Concepts that seemed harder to grasp in the past are now suddenly opened up and you begin to see how these unfold in front of your eyes.

Your thought process and thinking become clear. Clearer than it has been since before you started refocusing your thoughts. This clarity can help you put things into perspective and get a better idea of where to start when making big decisions in your life.

It helps you feel grounded and connected. Connected to who you are as an individual. Connected to the universe. Connected to those around you.

Other benefits

Better parenting

Some of the biggest benefits that parents can enjoy from meditation include being able to relax. Especially when frustration and anger build because things aren't going your way. The kids are driving you crazy. Tensions are beginning to build. You are desperately trying not to lose your temper or say something you might regret. Calm your mind and your negative thoughts with meditation. It can help with emotional stress you may be feeling.

Instead of spiraling down and hurting those you really care about (more often than not this is through a war of words,) you can short-circuit this tension by being able to regulate your mood by gaining greater clarity.

Reduced stress and anxiety

The exact opposite of stress and anxiety is peace and calm. How do you get there though? This may sound like it is out of reach within a short space of time, but the reality is that it doesn't have to take long to find that inner peace you've been searching for. Another huge benefit when it comes to meditation is that you don't need to spend money on fancy equipment. It's totally free. You can do it anywhere and at any time.

When it comes to stress and anxiety this is quite important because we all know that these emotions can strike at any time. You have the answer to reducing these emotional minefields by spending time clearing your mind, opening your heart and just being present in the moment.

Happier mindset

Let's face it, we live in a negative world. We are surrounded by negativity. All you have to do is read tabloid headlines, watch the news, and even just speak with others. All this negativity can be draining emotionally. A lot of this negativity comes from allowing ourselves to overthink everything. Thanks to the world we live in and our environment this is where our thoughts go automatically.

We can stop negative thinking in its tracks by practicing mindfulness techniques combined with meditation. It doesn't even need to take that long. What you may be thinking is, is this going to take years to master? (and that's why you've never done it before), it can actually be done by routinely focusing on becoming happier through daily meditation.

Remember to start off small. You can always move on from there. Your sessions can be lengthened over time. As you do begin to master this you will notice that your whole outlook on life begins to change.

Better relationships

Getting on with others can be tricky. There's no denying that because each of us is unique we have our own little quirks that make us who we are. These don't always work in our favor. Sometimes these differences can rub us or our significant other up the wrong way. What may have seemed cute or attractive at the beginning of a relationship can quickly turn into irritation.

Instead of allowing emotions to get the better of us and becoming upset, meditation can help control moods we may be experiencing. We can learn greater patience, understanding, and begin to accept those we have close relationships with more. It gives us the opportunity to really think about what we do. It highlights the actions we may be taking and how these actions affect those around us.

Part of improving relationships with others is understanding ourselves better. Meditation gives us the framework to be able to do this. It brings us into the present, allowing us to focus on what is happening now, rather than living in the past.

Increased productivity

As the world of work continues to change at lightning speed it becomes more and more challenging for individuals in the workplace to keep up. Not only keeping up but remaining sane in the process. Pressures in the workplace can easily turn a job you were extremely passionate about into something you just do for a paycheck at the end of each month. The truth is that if you don't do something about it there's a great chance that your current "tolerance" of your job can turn into "loathing."

You want to be able to keep that spark alive. To get the most out of your days and to wake up each morning excited for a brand-new day and the challenges you may face as you do what you love. Meditation can help you release unnecessary tension you may be feeling. If you happen to be worried or anxious about something we already know that meditation can bring you inner peace and harmony. It can help your thoughts become free of tension. It can help you relax.

Other ways meditation can benefit you in your work situation include:

- Allow you to discover creative solutions.
- Enhancing your energy levels.

- Improved ability to plan, figuring things out in your mind.

- Increase your concentration span.

Health

One of the most significant health benefits in this day and age is probably being able to overcome stress and anxiety. This practice helps us to ground ourselves in the present moment rather than wasting valuable energy dwelling on the past or worrying about what the future may bring. These emotions can directly be attributed to anxiety and can lead to a wide variety of health problems.

Meditation can help you deal with stress on a daily basis. Without meditation we can easily become totally overwhelmed by the amount of stress we are holding on to. Being able to decompress and release this tension. It's choosing not to let it accumulate.

According to London's Coventry University, lead researcher, Ivana Buric had this to say about a study performed in 2017 about the connection between meditation, inflammation, depression, cancer, mental, and physical health:

> Millions of people around the world already enjoy the health benefits of mind-body interventions like yoga or meditation, but what they perhaps don't realize is that these benefits begin at a molecular level and can change the way our genetic code goes about its business. (Cohut, 2019)

Meditation can have very real benefits when it comes to chronic pain relief. This is especially true of debilitating pain caused by rheumatoid arthritis, osteoarthritis and fibromyalgia. Techniques used in this type of meditation are based on cognitive behavioral therapy or CBT. A lot of this pain is caused by psychological pain—mindfulness meditation can short circuit this and help alleviate some of this hurt.

Additional health benefits might include:

- Help overcoming addiction.
- Mental agility.
- Control of impulsivity.

Patience

Yet another negative side effect to our living in the modern world. It is a world of instant gratification. We want what we want, and we want it now. There's no such thing as practicing patience anymore. Even our children have learned from an early age that they don't need to wait for anything. Whatever they want comes naturally and easily. We all know that while we are currently living our lives this way, it is actually against the law of the universe and the law of nature. For everything there is a time and season and we need to learn that in many instances we need to wait. Sure, we can always rush in, expecting a solution immediately but it's not to say that the solution we find right now at this moment is actually the best possible solution for us.

Meditation can teach us to control our urge for that sense of immediacy we have. Meditation can teach us that practicing patience is using wisdom. As we get older we actually do know deep down when patience is necessary. The opposite of patience is impulsivity. This reaction can get us into quite a bit of trouble. When we have a knee-jerk reaction to things people say or do. This can irreparably damage relationships.

Impulsivity can lead to financial woes as we make irrational buying decisions without thinking things through. We can overreact to situations we find ourselves in at home or in the workplace—the list goes on and on. In short, learning to be patient, even with yourself is way more beneficial. One final note when it comes to patience is that it is not simply being passive and waiting for things to happen. It is a form of self-discipline and control.

Confidence

Confidence can be broken down into two distinct parts. On one side confidence is measured and gained as you compare yourself with others in your field. This could be anything from parenthood to your actual vocation. How good are you when measured against these benchmarks? Your confidence will determine your choices and how you act in these situations.

The second type of confidence is internal. It is measured by how you feel about yourself when compared to those around you. Most of the time, this confidence is measured and judged by us. It just so happens that we are much harder on ourselves than others would be on us and this can make our self-esteem take a knock. We are really measuring our self-worth.

The world preys on the level of confidence we have. Without it we are bombarded with stuff that is supposed to make us feel better about ourselves. This should supposedly lead to greater self-confidence. The truth is that the only person's approval we should be after is our own. Sure, the world is screaming that we need to conform to this standard of acceptance or that standard of experience. However, we should only be benchmarking ourselves against ourselves and no-one else.

Meditation is one of the ways we can deal with this very real modern-day problem. Through meditation we get to connect with who we really are. Not on the surface, but deep within. It's here that we gain a clearer understanding of all that we are and all that we have to offer the world. Meditation allows us to "just be still." To focus on just one thing until we have perfect clarity. Mindfulness keeps us from being judgmental about who we are. About some of the things we have done, or maybe haven't done. You focus inward on yourself, rather than paying attention to those around you. Through meditation you get to process things that may have happened to you. Mindfulness will let you acknowledge these thoughts and simply let them go.

This isn't a quick fix or something that is going to happen overnight. In fact, chances are it is going to take a while for you to work through each limiting belief you may have of yourself. Meditation helps you separate what's real from the lies you've been telling yourself for ages. Meditation helps you to move from that place of perceived confidence to genuine confidence. This practice takes time and needs you to stick with it for it to take positive effect and make a long-lasting difference.

Peace

This is possibly one of the most sought-after reasons for meditation. Let's face it, the world has gone crazy and because of this constant, frenetic pace it is easy for us to get caught up in the madness. Our minds are crammed so full of the things of the world and peace is not one of them. We don't need to feel so tightly wound or take on all the lack of tolerance and injustice of the world. Finding inner peace is possible.

A lot of people are under the impression that for you to have peace in your life you need to be quiet. While a peaceful environment may very well be calm, soothing, or quiet, this doesn't have to be so for you to develop an internal peace. For a moment think about how tumultuous the ocean can be. Yet even with these forces of nature you can gain an inner peace and tranquility. For some it is as simple as rain that's falling rhythmically. Or the smell after the rain.

You can discover peace anywhere. It doesn't mean searching in silence. Peace comes with breathing. Focusing our energy on controlling how we do this can help us alter our state of mind. Peace comes through feeling secure. Feeling and knowing that you are loved. You are wanted, you matter. Meditation can help you recognize these gifts. It can help you realize that you have had these things all along, you just haven't realized it yet.

Visualize yourself being in a place that makes you feel tranquil and peaceful. Whether this is a sunset, a walk through the forest, watching the sunrise over the sea, hiking through the mountains, or simply sitting contemplating nature and the universe. Discovering inner peace through meditation is possible and you don't need to be on a yoga mat or at an expensive retreat to enjoy this.

Strength

We can have the desire to develop different types of strength to help us through various stages of our lives. There are times when we need actual physical strength, inner strength to possibly deal with mental or emotional challenges. Other forms of strength include resilience. That ability to bounce back whenever faced with a challenge.

Inner strength is what helps you move through life's challenges without getting stuck. The world and everything around us is constantly moving, growing, changing. Are we tenacious enough to move with these changes? Inner strength gives us internal resources we need. Emotional characteristics to help us face things that may test our ability to withstand challenges.

Strength can be divided into mental- physical- and emotional health and wellness. By working on one of these aspects we actually benefit the other two because they are interlinked. Some of the benefits of developing inner strength through meditation include:

- It reduces the amount of stress we may be feeling by calming the mind.
- We can regulate our emotions.
- Our consciousness can be drawn to focus on the present.
- The importance of tenacity can be emphasized.
- We can reflect on situations, ponder, and respond appropriately.
- It gives us the opportunity to shift our thinking.
- We can develop positive habits.

Inner strength gives us the ability to thrive rather than merely getting by. Being able to discover, develop, or tap into this inner strength is something that will also take practice and time. Meditation and mindfulness can help us build these characteristics that we can use throughout our lives.

Focus

Imagine how great it would be if you could simply do things without being distracted. You could begin a task and see it all the way through without having intrusive thoughts or distractions pulling you away from what needs to be done.

With improved focus you can become a better listener, a better thinker, and better at planning. Each of these characteristics come with benefits. You can save yourself a whole lot of time by not having to clear your mind of unnecessary thoughts. An increased attention span improves your awareness of the present. Awareness of this moment rather than those of the past. Knowing what needs to be done can help minimize stress.

That overly-busy brain of ours can potentially be altered to concentrate on those things that are important and necessary. Meditation allows us to rid ourselves of unnecessary distractions. Before trying any of these things it should be noted that none of these things are going to magically appear. As with anything in life, if you want to become good at it you need to practice. Meditation is no different to this.

Increase mindfulness awareness. This can help you deal with one thing at a time. Shift your focus and channel all your energy into one specific direction. By doing so you can become more productive than ever before. You can get more done because you are working on just one task at a time. Feeling out of control is as a result of an over-active, busy mind. Mindfulness is what will allow you to acknowledge the thought, and let it go without spending unnecessary time and energy on it.

If you find yourself battling to concentrate on important things, you may want to give guided meditation a go. Chapter 7 is dedicated specifically to this type of meditation. You can scan through each of the topics and find the one that is likely to improve your concentration skills.

Sleep

Stress is possibly the number one reason for people battling with insomnia or other sleep disorders. Depression and anxiety are contributing factors to sleep irregularities. It may be true that as you get older you need less sleep than while you are still growing, however, this doesn't mean not being able to sleep at all.

Meditation can have a positive effect on your overall sense of peace and tranquility. This is what is often lacking and the cause of us not being able to get the amount of rest our bodies need. It stands to reason that because meditation helps reduce stress, while increasing peace and tranquility, sleep patterns can improve.

Meditation can help us relax, which is exactly what we need to be able to enjoy a peaceful night's rest. From a physiological perspective, meditation can help with the production of hormones necessary for sleep. Through regulated breathing you can control your heart rate allowing your body to relax enough to enjoy undisturbed sleep for longer. The secret to successful sleep meditation is the ability to calm and quieten the mind.

Appearance

Believe it or not, our current lifestyle (without meditation) takes its toll on our physical appearance. Stress from everyday life wreaks havoc on our bodies, affecting things like circulation, wrinkles, aging, dry skin, and hair loss to name a few. While some may argue that each of these things can be attributed to getting older, the truth is that this can be reversed.

The state of our lives and getting caught up in daily activities can rob us of taking the time we should in paying attention to ourselves physically. As a result, we don't eat correctly. We follow a diet of fast food or processed foods. We flip flop between diet fads which mess with the body's digestive system. We don't exercise quite as much as we should, if at all. Instead of increasing our water intake we replace this with caffeine. Once again, stress is in the thick of things.

The secret to looking and feeling younger can be found in regular meditation. It helps us to relax more, sleep better, clearing our minds of anxiety and worry we may be experiencing. Deep breathing or breathing correctly provides the body with vital oxygen that is necessary for healthy skin. Instead of fatigue there is renewed energy. Skin is revitalized because toxins are released. You will also find yourself drinking more water rather than needing all the "pick me ups" of caffeine.

Decision-making

As part of the 40,000 or so thoughts passing through our minds each day we seldom realize how many decisions we have to make. A lot of these are done on autopilot. Think about how many decisions you have made today alone. Did you choose to get up the moment the alarm went off or did you choose to hit snooze? You had to make a decision about what to wear. How long did this take you and how many times did you actually change your mind? Water, tea or coffee? Cereal or toast?

What type of meditation routine are you going to follow today? Which affirmation should you choose? Do you wake your spouse or let them sleep in a little longer—they worked later than usual last night? Which route do you take going to work? Do you stop for gas?

All of this and you've only been awake for an hour or so... Can you see how many choices and decisions we face constantly. No wonder we often feel so overwhelmed by decisions we have to make that we simply don't make any decisions. Of course, this can become an endless cycle if we can't come to terms with the fact that decision-making is very much part of who we are and life in general.

Meditation benefits us by allowing us to see things more clearly. Making decisions with a clear mind. Being able to focus on what is needed rather than what we want right now. It can help us feel more confident and assured. Being clear and focused can help us make wise decisions that will be to our benefit long term. Having your mind already made up, when faced with a decision you have already made, there's no having to weigh the pros and cons. A clear mind eases pressure that often goes hand in hand with decision-making. It reduces the stress, panic, and fear of making the wrong decision. Meditation gives you the tools to use rational thought to come up with the right solution.

NOTES

Chapter 6: The Importance of a Daily Routine

> *"So much time and effort is spent on wanting to change, trying to change, to be somebody different, better, or new. Why not use this time to get comfortable with yourself as you are instead?"*
>
> ~ Andy Puddicombe (Headspace, 2021)

The importance of creating a routine that's right for you is one thing. Being able to stick with it is something completely different. I think that by now you would have realized that it is going to take practice. Something you need to set aside enough time for. You will need to be resilient in your resolve to follow your routine each day, regardless of whatever else is going on in your life.

Making excuses is easy. The challenge is doing what you have committed to do—routinely. It is carving out that time that may seem like a sacrifice, because let's face it, we can all find reasons not to do those things that are really important. Guaranteed, if you look hard enough, you will always find reasons for not sticking with your routine. Especially when you are just starting out. This is the most crucial time of all. It is getting past those first couple of weeks. Moving beyond the amount of time it takes to create a habit, it takes discipline and dedication. Characteristics that not everyone possesses. It can however be learned.

Firstly, please understand that there are many different routines that you can establish in your life. Some routines are specifically directed toward health and fitness, a routine for work, study, family, community service, and even personal development. How many of these routines are actually there to help you connect with who you are as a person? Most are focused on the physical, even those that need mental acuity. Most routines have a goal. If there's no end result in mind then it's worth asking yourself what's the point? Why are you doing what you are doing? Have you even given this some serious thought? What is motivating you to go down this path?

Routines are important because they give us daily patterns to follow. Structure. They help us achieve the things we really want out of life in the simplest possible way. This is still not to say that getting there isn't going to take work, because it is. Developing a routine that you have enough willpower to follow and stick to takes planning and dedication. Sometimes it may be uncomfortable and that's okay. There may be days when you fail. That's quite alright. Just be certain that you find the motivation to get going again.

Why meditation should be part of your daily routine

Before coming up with a workable strategy that will get you to the point where your meditation becomes second nature to you, you need to figure out why you want this.

What is it about meditation that will improve your day? Are you clear enough with the genuine benefits of meditation or do you see it merely as a short-term solution? Is it something you're doing because it's all that everyone's talking about so you're going to give it a go? If it doesn't work within a couple of days you can always return to what you have been doing—nothing!

Your reason for choosing to meditate daily needs to be something you can identify with. It shouldn't be something you want to do because your best friend is trying it out too. You, and only you need to be the driving force behind really working at this, otherwise it is never going to benefit you. Ask yourself some of the following questions to determine your motivation behind this habit.

- Are you meditating to unwind and decompress from stressors throughout the day?
- Do you want to become better prepared for the day ahead of you?
- Is it something you need to improve, maybe your mental or emotional well-being?
- Are you looking for effective ways to control your moods?
- Do you want to improve your ability to concentrate?

Each of these are just some of the benefits to meditation. Our inability to control our thoughts to process the increased stress we experience daily can lead to other unhealthy lifestyle choices. Things like eating incorrectly, becoming addicted to alcohol, drugs, and anything else that could be destructive. It's easy to understand why this happens when you can't get your mind and thinking under control. You are less inclined to make wise, healthy decisions.

Developing or sticking with a daily routine isn't easy in the beginning. You want to develop habits that are going to benefit not only you but those around you too. Something worth mentioning is that trying to develop any form of a new routine is going to have its challenges and obstacles to try and prevent you from achieving those things you want to achieve.

Tips to create positive habits

Here are a number of ways you can do this. Try following some of these guidelines to incorporate this new routine into your day.

Know exactly what you want

What is it that you are trying to achieve? You have to know what you want out of this routine? Decide what, and why meditation is important to you. Once you know this you will have a starting point. A solid foundation for you to work from.

What's the plan?

As with anything in your life you need a plan. Some direction of where it is that you want to go. Without this there can be no routine. It goes back to understanding what you want to achieve ultimately. Once you know this you can develop a path to get there. What are the things you need to prioritize before you begin? What do you have to work with? It's all great wanting to implement a meditation routine but do you know where you want to do this? How much time do you have available? How do you plan to work around emergencies? Can you see that once you begin to break it down there are a lot of much smaller components that need to be considered.

Decide beforehand

Piggybacking on planning is making decisions beforehand. We face hundreds, if not thousands of micro-decisions each day. Most of these are sub-conscious and automatic. You don't need to think about them. The thing about making a decision about something is that once your mind or intention is set, whenever the thought or question crosses your mind, you don't need to go through the whole mental process of weighing in all the pros and cons (and this all happens within seconds).

You have already decided so facing the challenge or obstacle becomes easy. Despite this mental tug-o-war taking place sub-consciously and quickly, it can still lead to mental fatigue. One of the things you are trying to eliminate through meditation.

Build on your goals

Your ability to break things down will help you map that pathway to get there. Don't try to do too much too soon. It is natural to want to dive right in and get things perfect from the get-go. While it is natural it is unrealistic. Starting off small should be the goal. Set small objectives you know you can achieve. Don't plan to meditate for an hour a day. This would be the big goal. The end goal. Right now, you might set the goal to practice mindfulness for five minutes each morning.

You are probably reading this and thinking to yourself, "That's too easy!" Many individuals who have been meditating for years, will tell you that being able to clear your mind of unnecessary thinking can take a lot longer than you realize. You want to develop a habit. This comes little by little and day-by-day.

Consistency is key

There's a reason why they call it a routine. You need to be consistent in your timing, and in your actions. Part of the reason behind the recommendation of establishing this routine first thing in the morning is you get to do it before the busyness of the day becomes a reality. Leaving this until later is way more likely going to result in procrastination. It becomes easier to find excuses for putting things off. Negative thinking creeps in and takes over. Whatever you do, stick with it. Do whatever it takes to keep your motivation levels high enough to get you over the procrastination hurdles.

Assess your progress

Every couple of days, weeks, or months, take your meditation temperature. How are things going? How are you feeling? What are the benefits you are getting out of this change in your lifestyle? As you begin to feel or see progress in your life daily, it becomes a motivating factor for you to keep at it.

Benefits of looking forward to "ME" time

The problem with reading the above statement is that whenever we think of doing something that's just for ourselves we feel guilty about it. We feel as though we are being selfish and because of this we choose not to focus on ourselves. The question then is, if you aren't prepared to pay attention to yourself and your own needs, how do you expect to be able to support those that rely on you?

There is a well-known saying that you cannot pour water from an empty cup. For your cup to be filled enough to share with others you have to think of yourself first. Do you know what you need to be able to get through the day or face down a specific challenge? It is not just these couple of benefits that can be felt immediately, take a look at some of these. They may just help you recognize how meditation and mindfulness can change your life.

Famous French philosopher from the 1600s, Blaise Pascal said that "All man's miseries derive from not being able to sit quietly in a room alone." (Sharma, 2014). If we think that this is a modern problem, this statement literally tells us that we have always seemed to be fighting this inner struggle to simply be still.

No special equipment necessary

You don't need to be limited to a specific area, room, venue, or need fancy equipment to be able to meditate. You simply need a quiet space. A place that is light and airy. Somewhere that you can be alone, undisturbed, for a set period of time. It is not going to cost you any money to begin meditating—all you need to do is begin.

Develop empathy and compassion

This is possibly one of the biggest benefits you can get out of meditation. It can help you become acutely aware of what is going on around you. You can gain a better insight into how those around you are feeling. Being mindful of them can help you become more understanding toward them. You may develop compassion and empathy toward those that may be experiencing challenges. So, how is this going to benefit you? It helps you release those "feel good" hormones. Instead of feeling stress and frustration you can open your heart to others.

Deal with stress and anxiety

This may be one of the greatest benefits of all. Stress and anxiety go hand-in-hand with the lifestyle of living in this day and age. Everything happens at lightning speed and we try to keep up with everything happening around us. The more we try and keep up the greater the chances are that we are likely to fall behind. This leads to even more stress and anxiety. We feel the pressure of facing deadlines, meeting targets, being everything for everybody. There is only so much of this kind of pressure that anyone can take. Much like a pressure cooker, there needs to be a release valve that allows you to let off enough steam to function again. Meditation can help identify this pressure valve. It can help you manage the amount of stress and anxiety you are under. It will never get rid of stress and anxiety.

This is just part of life. It can, however, give you coping mechanisms. Being able to reduce these two emotions, and deal with them more effectively can improve both mental and physical health.

Regulate blood pressure

Another health benefit is being able to regulate your blood pressure. The breathing exercises that form a major part of meditation increase oxygen levels in your bloodstream. This in turn can decrease blood pressure. The health benefits of this is not just reducing the strain on the heart. It can reduce the risks of strokes and even heart attacks. Meditation increases relaxation which reduces tension throughout the body. Earlier we spoke of the fight or flight response we are each born with. Meditation can help regulate this response.

Awareness of self

Meditation can help you discover who you are. You can gain a better understanding of who you are and why you do the things you do. Self-reflection isn't always easy. It is being able to see ourselves for who we are. Accepting the bad along with the good. As you begin to understand who you are, you can gain a better insight into how you react or interact with those around you. Once you understand who you are you can gain greater clarity and awareness of where your thoughts are taking you. Are they destructive or positive? Being able to recognize what you are thinking gives you control over those thoughts. You can shift your focus from negative to positive.

Improved outlook on life

This works directly with our emotional and mental wellbeing. Instead of seeing things as being doom and gloom, or having a glass half-full outlook, it can reduce stress, anxiety, and depression. By focusing on positive outcomes, you would have to replace negative thinking. Too much negativity can result in depression, making it much more difficult to turn this mood around. You would probably have noticed by now that when you are focused on everything that's wrong, that's all that seems to perpetuate in your life—negative rather than positive.

There are way more benefits to being able to spend quality time with yourself. Take some time out and make some notes as to why this is important to you. What benefits are you looking for? How would your life change if you got to experience some of the things mentioned above?

NOTES

Chapter 7: Guided Meditations

"You must learn to get in touch with the innermost essence of your being. This true essence is beyond the ego. It is fearless; it is free; it is immune to criticism; it does not fear any challenge. It is beneath no one, superior to no one, and full of magic, mystery, and enchantment."

~ Deepak Chopra (The Editors at Chopra.com, 2018)

Getting into the habit of practicing meditation or mindfulness on a regular basis is made so much easier by making use of guided meditation techniques. What's the difference between normal meditation and guided meditation? Firstly, guided meditation is a whole lot easier because you don't need to really sit and think about what to do next, where to set your thoughts or your focus because you have a narrator or guide telling you what to do. It's so much easier than for you to come up with something on your own.

Having someone guide you through meditative steps helps you gain the right focus to heal yourself emotionally, mentally, and even physically. It lets you focus on what you should be concentrating on rather than mentally trying to think about what you need to do next.

Of course, there's nothing wrong with putting your own meditations together. As a matter of fact, once you've been using some of the guided meditation techniques that follow you may have your own ideas of those things that really work for you, or what resonates with you. There may be some techniques in the guided motivations that you find particularly challenging and you need to change. Give it a bit of time until you feel comfortable and once you get there you can start putting your own "guided meditation" together.

Listening to a narrator guiding and instructing you can help you relax both your mind and body before directing you toward much deeper meditation. It can also stop you from feeling completely overwhelmed by starting this new practice.

Something rather interesting is that the brain cannot tell the difference between what is real and what you imagine. It stands to reason that if this is true it's easy to discover the benefits of meditation on the brain. This can possibly help you recognize and experience the benefits of meditation a lot sooner than trying it on your own. It can also make it less frustrating for you.

Before you begin

By now you should have identified what time of day is going to be best for you. Is it early in the morning before the kids and the rest of the household wake? A fixed time when things are peaceful. Maybe evenings are better once you are done with dinner. Everything is done, the kids are bathed, asleep in bed, and the house is quiet once more. Choosing the right time is one that works for you. Both of these times have distinct benefits. Early morning meditation sets you up for the day. It can help you feel like you can scale any mountain or face any obstacle throughout the day.

Evenings on the other hand can help you unwind, destress, and settle both mind and body shortly before even attempting sleep. For those battling with insomnia, this is often a much better time of day to get into the habit of meditating.

There are loads of guided meditations out there, from audio, YouTube videos, and specialty meditation blogs and websites. There are podcasts, actual meditation (yoga) studios that can help you. For more information check out the resources chapter that follows below.

For now, let's take a closer look at several guided meditations you can begin to implement in your life right now—today! You don't need to wait, buy fancy equipment, or invest a fortune in something you are just starting with.

Start off small. Begin with much shorter meditations until you are comfortable with the process. The more time you invest in this practice, the more you're likely to strengthen your core, supporting good posture and the ability to sit comfortably for longer. Aim to get a couple of minutes each day initially. Look at anywhere between five minutes to half an hour. Your ultimate goal should be around an hour. That's if it is time you can spare.

There's no point in meditating if you can't work through a step-by-step practice session without feeling guilty. In the back of your mind, you might be stressed out about work at the office, a deadline, a recent argument with your spouse, finances, health, or anything else. Worrying about these things will interfere with a successful meditation session.

There's a pretty long list of things you can meditate on. A list of these might include the following:

- Mindfulness meditation

- Breathing – counting your breath exercise*

- Focused meditation
- Body scan
- Visualization
- Sleep
- Health issues – Lowering blood pressure, dealing with ongoing illness etc.
- A quick blast for a quick fix
- Managing anxiety and stress
- Handling the pressure of examinations, tests, reviews, etc.
- Focus, confidence and self-esteem
- Dealing with grief, anger, and frustration
- Gratitude
- Healthy relationships
- Procrastination

Before you begin

Irrespective of the type of meditation you want to use, there are a couple of things you need to be aware of. Things that should possibly be on a checklist before you begin your meditative process.

The main aim of any meditation is being able to shift between being awake and present in the moment. In a state where you are aware, yet so relaxed and comfortable that the words can wash over you. That place where you are filled with peace, joy, and happiness.

Knowing what you want to achieve before you even begin meditating is another vital step. Some call this part having a goal or setting out with a clear picture of what you want to achieve from your meditation. It is not easy or beneficial just going into a meditative state with no goal in mind. This part of preparation is called setting your intention. Know what you want to have happen by the end of the process.

- What do you want to experience?
- How would you like to feel?

Rather than just going through the motions, making use of guided meditation places your mind and body into a relaxed state. One where you can forget about all those things that are going on around you. Engaging in the present time, moment-by-moment. You can use this technique to target specific parts of the body that are tense or sore. Relaxing them relieves you of the everyday pressures of life. Meditation places you in a physical place. Decide on the feeling you desire in the end.

Physical preparation

Here are a couple of things you need to consider before you begin meditating. These things should be constant. i.e., stuff you should do each time you meditate.

No matter the style of meditation you've chosen. This is common to each. Find a quiet place to meditate. The environment needs to be right.

Be sure that your environment is best suited to your meditation. Some people prefer very bright, airy spaces where there is plenty of natural sunlight, a breeze that can blow into and through the room.

For others, the room should be light enough to be able to see, but dimly lit so that burning candles can be seen.

Is your clothing loose enough for you to feel comfortable? Anything that is tight, or elastic is noticeable, needs to be replaced with something flowing instead.

For seated meditation, be sure that you have cushions, a yoga mat, or other piece of furniture you can lean on for support if absolutely necessary. You need to be comfortable enough for between five minutes to half an hour remaining in the same position.

Be sure you aren't going to be interrupted or disturbed during your meditation. Find the time to meditate more or less at the same time daily. Sometimes your spouse, significant other, and other family members should be made aware of your schedule. Asking for this quiet time or alone time is not being selfish. You are actually doing it to benefit both themselves and you. Close the door and keep a "do not disturb" sign handy.

You can also eliminate unnecessary distractions by switching off your mobile phone. Don't simply put it on silent, "just in case there's an emergency." Guaranteed, it can wait for a couple of minutes. Think about it for a moment—are you more- or less-likely to move into that meditative state without distractions.

Absolute no- no's

For guided meditation to be effective you need to be fully alert and engaged in the process. Call it being invested in each moment. Stay away from this type of meditation if you need to pay attention to what you are doing. An example of this would be putting dinner in the oven and then choosing to meditate.

In all likelihood you are going to have burnt food, burnt pots, an oven that now smells foul and you don't have an edible meal to boot.

Don't meditate if you should be watching your children. That is, leaving them to their own devices. In all probability your meditation session will be interrupted, maybe even several times… Instead of finding that inner calm and peace, you find yourself worrying about what they might be up to. Schedule your meditation sessions for when the kids are still asleep, or you know there is a responsible adult there to supervise them.

A definite no-no for meditation is while driving. Some people like to listen to these "soothing sounds" on their way to work or driving kids to school. Because of the relaxing effects of guided meditation, it may just lead to drowsiness, or deep relaxation where you don't have all your faculties about you. If you need to be alert and focused you are most definitely not going to be at your best during this practice.

Driving mindfully is an activity rather than a meditation technique. There are distinctive benefits to being able to do this. Some of these include improved concentration and focus. Think about it as if you are giving yourself a running commentary of the route you are traveling. Or what driving actually entails (each action necessary.) Some of these would include the way you hold the steering wheel, how you judge the distance between you and other cars on the road. When and where you need to indicate and how to do this. How you check your rearview, and side mirrors. These are just some of the basics. Although not being meditative, you can definitely make use of this in a mindful way.

Here are guided meditations for each of these:

Mindfulness meditation

> *"Mindfulness is simply being aware of what is happening right now without wishing it were different; enjoying the pleasant without holding on when it changes (which it will); being with the unpleasant without fearing it will always be this way (which it won't)."*
>
> *~ James Baraz (Good Reads, n.d.)*

Seasoned professional meditation practitioners will still go through dips. They can't always be high because that's how life today is being wrapped up and packaged with a neat bow. We aren't meant to think for ourselves. Being able to meditate mindfully means tuning out the world and concentrating only on what is. Right at this moment.

Beginning of Mindfulness Meditation

Are you ready? Are you comfortable? Let us begin.

Choose the best position for you to meditate in. You may find it easier lying down. If this is for you then lie on your back, arms by your side in a relaxed, comfortable position. Keep your legs fully extended yet relaxed. You might want to support the small of your back, or your knees with a pillow. Adjust your body position until you are completely comfortable.

Close your eyes—gently. Quieten your thoughts and your mind.

Breathing

Concentrate on your breathing. Notice how you inhale through your nose. Your lungs are now filled with fresh air.

As you exhale, notice how your stomach deflates. Let the air escape through your mouth. Make a "shhh" sound like air being released by a tire or a balloon.

Breathe in. Notice how your lungs fill and touch gently against your rib cage. This may come across as a tightening of your tummy.

Breathe out. Slowly, breathe out through your mouth, lips together, making the shhh ing sound.

Breathe in deeply.

Exhale.

Imagine you are breathing in vital, life-giving energy. Visualize it as a pure white light.

Just relax.

Pay attention to each breath as it enters your lungs.

You are feeling calm and relaxed with each breath in, and out.

Each breath out carries with it any negative energy you may be holding on to.

Breathe in, and out. In, and out. Focus completely on your breathing. It is happening quite naturally, as it should. In, and out. In, and out.

Continue to breathe in and out... naturally

Check in with Your Body

How is your body feeling at this moment?

Allow each thought to come to mind. Acknowledge it and let it go.

Feel the rhythm of your heart beating?

Pay close attention to the way each part of your body feels.

Is there pain?

Are you feeling relaxed?

Don't do anything to change the sensations you are feeling.

Acknowledge them and move onto another part of your body.

Slowly focus on your thoughts. What are you thinking about?

As each thought crosses your mind, see it as if you were sitting in a grand theater. You are just there to watch. The stage is set. Each thought will come to center stage.

Take a look at it without passing judgment or focusing on one thought for too long. Let it move across the stage that is really your mind. Don't hang onto it or keep it on your mind's stage for longer than absolutely necessary.

Release each one and let them go. Don't judge yourself or make up any preconceived notions about your thinking.

View each of these thoughts as exactly that. A thought.

How is your body feeling?

Keep checking in with yourself, each time taking a few moments to notice any emotions you may be experiencing. Let these go.

Through this time your thoughts may return to the past.

Perhaps you are thinking about the future.

Gently, rein these thoughts in and bring them back to here and now.

There is no moment that is more important than right now.

Return to being more aware of your breathing once more.

Feel how the oxygen fills your lungs.

Breathe in light and energy.

Breathe out negativity.

Breathe in light and energy.

Breathe out negativity.

Focus on each breath.

All you need to concern yourself with is here, right now, at this moment.

Closing Your Meditation

Slowly, return your breathing to normal.

Concentrate on how calm you are feeling. You have released each thought, feeling, and emotion that has been damaging. You are feeling at peace.

You are feeling full of energy and vitality.

When you are ready, open your eyes. Slowly return to the present.

Begin with your feet and slowly stretch each part of your body. Follow this same thinking until you have reached the tips of each of your fingers.

You can sit up and return to the here and now.

Breathing – and counting your breath exercise

> *"When life is foggy, path is unclear and mind is dull, remember your breath. It has the power to give you peace. It has the power to resolve the unsolved equations of life."*
>
> ~ Amit Ray (Good Reads, n.d.-b)

The search has long been on to find ways to get rid of daily pressures, stress, and anxiety that come hand-in-hand with the modern world we live in. Everything seems out of control and most of the time they are because we are. We battle to get even the basics right. The exciting thing is that something as simple as breathing can be the answer to all the pressure we are feeling.

The secret, like most forms of meditation, is being able to master the art of focusing on the here and now. Being present. Being mindful and using techniques that are absolutely free. The only cost to ourselves, a bit of time. As we make wise decisions to invest this time in ourselves we can begin to see results. One of the oldest and simplest forms of meditation recorded, it is just as effective today as it was in ancient times.

Preparation Before You Begin

As with most meditation exercises, the environment you choose to meditate in can have a marked effect on the success of your meditation. Our surroundings can prove to be disruptive, breaking our much-needed concentration. Finding the right space to meditate cannot be overstressed. Something not mentioned till now is that any form of distraction is going to vie for your attention. This doesn't simply mean a small space that's bright and airy. It also speaks to an environment that is free of noise, distractions, electronic equipment, and anything else that might demand your attention.

With breathing meditation, it is important to sit in an upright, comfortable position. The actual position for this meditation needs to be well supported. Both feet should be firmly planted on the ground, back upright, knees bent at a 90° angle. If you choose to sit on a cushion the same directions apply. Chances are you will need several cushions to achieve the same result.

Beginning of Breathing Meditation

If you are comfortable and free of all distractions it's time for us to begin:

This meditation is way more effective when your eyes are closed. It helps cut out visual cues that may distract you, drawing your attention away from your breathing.

As you begin I want you to pay close attention to what we call "mindful breathing." What this really is, is focusing all your energy throughout this meditation on your breath. We all breathe throughout the day. Most of the time it is something we don't have to think about. This meditation is going to teach you just that. The benefits of being able to focus on each breath you take has many healing properties. Some of these include your ability to decrease your stress levels, dealing with anxiety and depression, and reducing negative thinking. You can also use this technique to help you focus better.

Begin by doing a couple of deep breathing exercises.

Take a deep breath, filling your lungs. You can count to three as you do this. Breathe through your nose.

Hold this breath for the slow count of two. (two seconds).

Slowly, breathe out through your mouth. Take another four seconds to do this.

Repeat this exercise until you have done five of these in total.

Check in with Your Body

Next, return your breathing to normal. However, you are not going to be extremely mindful of each breath you inhale, and exactly how you exhale.

How do each of these actions make you feel?

Focus on specific sensation you may be experiencing as you breathe.

How do your nostrils feel?

Is the air you are breathing in through your nostrils feeling warm or cold. Your nasal passages will feel this by either feeling cool or warm. The first place you will feel this will be the sides of your nostrils. As the air moves up the nose, notice how it hits your nasal passages before passing downward toward your lungs.

Notice how your chest rises as the oxygen fills your lungs.

The moment your thoughts begin to wander, guide them back to focus on your breathing—gently.

You are beginning to relax. Now it is time for you to pay attention to how your body feels.

Notice how your back feels as it rests against the back of the chair. You are seated upright. You are comfortable. As you pay close attention to your back, notice if there is any tension in the muscles. Are you feeling any pain or discomfort? If you do, release the tension or discomfort and move on.

Work your way down your body.

What do your legs feel like? Are they feeling heavy? Is there any tension or resistance to your wanting to relax? Focus on these muscles, loosening and releasing any stiffening.

Can you feel how each of your feet is touching the floor? Connecting with the ground beneath you.

Feel energy and vibrations flowing through your body.

As you work through each area of your body, pay attention to whenever you feel that tenderness or resistance.

Just breathe.

Continue through each part of your body, repeat the same process.

Your shoulders, arms, wrists, hands, fingers. You may need to clench your fists and release them for each of your fingers to relax.

Move onto your face. Are you tensing muscles, clenching your jaw, tightening your cheeks or mouth? Relax and release these negative emotions, or anything else that you may be thinking negatively toward.

Go back to thinking about your breathing.

Notice how it is quite natural.

Inhale, exhale. Inhale, exhale.

Each breath should be natural.

Count each of your breaths. Inhaling and exhaling forms one breathing cycle. Pay close attention how effortlessly and automatically each breathing cycle follows closely to the next. The motion is seamless.

What does each breath feel like as it passes through the body?

Pull that wandering mind back gently. It is going to move off topic rapidly unless you can notice when this happens. Repeat the words "breathing.") By now you should have a simple yet effective way to release any unwanted thoughts.

Continue focusing on your breathing by counting in cycles of ten. Breathing in, and out mindfully becomes one cycle. Repeat, "One" in your mind and so on.) Count each breath cycle till you reach ten and then begin again at one.

Keep this up for between five and ten minutes.

Focus on your breathing only. Pull your mind and thoughts back gently if it wanders. Don't get upset when this happens, it is natural.

Repeat your body scan process.

Beginning with your back.

Your chest and body, your hips, your legs, your knees, your calves and lower legs.

Pay attention to your feet that are grounded.

Move toward your shoulders, your upper arms, elbow, lower arms.

Wrists, hands, fingers.

Neck, head, face, eyes, nose, mouth.

Notice how you are now feeling much more relaxed than you were earlier on.

Be mindful of each part of your body and then your body as a whole.

Closing Your Meditation

Give thanks and gratitude for being able to complete this exercise.

Return to your breathing.

You can now begin to open your eyes and return to your conscious state.

Walking meditation

> *"You have feet, and if you don't make use of them it's a loss and a waste. Someone is telling you now so that in the future you cannot say: 'No one told me that it was important to enjoy using my feet.'"*
>
> ~ Thich Nhat Hahn (Famous Quotes & Sayings, n.d.)

For this next meditation routine, we are going to use a technique that isn't used as often as it could be. There are loads of different types of meditation that can be done while walking. Some of these include being more mindful, reducing anxiety and stress through breathing, getting in touch with your emotions, and simply becoming one with nature. Expressing gratitude for things you have around you.

Preparation Before You Begin

The preparation for this type of meditation is rather simple. Be sure you are wearing comfortable clothes, suited to walking. This would include the right kind of shoes. Find somewhere to walk that is not going to be too distracting. You may want to find an open field; an open park; a forest; a beach; somewhere in the mountains—it needs to be relatively flat so you aren't likely to trip and fall over rocks. Perhaps you have a nice, peaceful garden. If you have pets, try and remove them for the length of your meditation. Your main aim is to minimize as many distractions as possible.

This meditation needs to be done with your eyes open. You need to be able to concentrate on a number of things at the same time. Preferably without having your surroundings interfere with how you go about using this technique. Being alert is one of the keys to this being successful.

The main aim with this meditation is to become more aware of your body. How it feels. How it reacts to its surroundings. This is still done in a mindful way. Not getting caught up too much on the physical, but simple awareness and then letting go.

The thing about walking is that because it is an activity we do completely automatically we seldom focus on this. Our minds are filled with everything by being caught up in past memories, current circumstances, and future worries. We lose out on being able to connect. Connecting with who we are. Connecting with our bodies and connecting with our surroundings. During this practice you want to get your mind to work in perfect harmony with your body. Through this you have the ability to become more mindful of the beauty that surrounds us. The feelings and emotions within us, and how your body feels each step of the way.

Beginning of Walking Meditation

Instead of focusing on each breath we take in, and how it feels as we empty our lungs during the exhale process, you are going to pay close attention to each step you take. Each step you take as you walk is done according to a rhythm. It is this rhythm you want to become aware of.

You set the pace of your walk. It doesn't really matter whether you are taking a brisk walk or a gentle stroll. You can tailor your awareness to match your movement.

Spend a minute or so on each part of the exercise.

Check in with Your Body

Begin walking.

Is your body feeling light as a feather or heavy as though you are weighed down?

Do your muscles feel relaxed, or are you feeling tense? A lot of this tension may be felt especially in your neck and shoulder muscles.

Are you walking with your shoulders hunched over, or is your back straight, shoulders back, and head held high?

Pay attention to how you are walking. Don't change anything. Just be aware, or mindful of each stride you take.

What is happening around you?

Are there children playing?

Is there a gentle breeze blowing?

Are there waves crashing against the rocks, seagulls flying overhead?

Don't focus all your attention on what you see. Simply acknowledge these things are happening and let them go.

What can you hear?

Can you hear the wind rushing through the forest, leaves blowing in the breeze?

As you walk, are dry leaves cracking beneath your feet?

Are birds chirping, or squawking?

Can you hear the laughter of children?

The squeaking of chain links from a swing?

Once again, recognize that these noises are there, but don't focus on them. Be mindful and let each sound go.

What can you smell?

Can you smell the distinct pine smell in the forest?

The dustiness of an open field. Perhaps it is the smell of freshly cut grass.

Maybe the freshness of recent rainfall.

Perhaps you can smell the saltiness of the sea, or the not so pleasant smell of fish or pollution washed onto the shore.

Many smells will remind us of previous experiences. Gently pull back your thoughts to become present and aware of the moment. Return to now.

How are you feeling?

Is the wind tousling your hair?

Can you feel the sunlight on your skin?

Is it making you feel hot, or simply warm?

Perhaps there is a light spray from the waves.

If you are walking on a beach, what does the sand feel like between your toes? Is the sand hot and dry or are you walking close to the shore where it is squishing between your toes?

Notice how your feet are connected to the earth. How your heel touches the ground followed by the sole, the ball of your foot, and finally your toes.

Observe, acknowledge, and let go.

What else is going on with your body?

Are your arms swinging in the same rhythm as your legs?

Notice how you are walking at a steady pace now.

Use these last few techniques to help ground yourself.

You know that your thoughts are going to drift and wander in every direction. Use the awareness of body movement to bring them back again.

Closing Your Meditation

Breathe normally, focus your attention on how the body moves as you walk.

Count each step cycle – this would begin using your right foot, followed through with your left. This represents one cycle. Your mind begins to focus on counting each movement. It is in tune with each step cycle. Being aware, your thoughts are in sync with the rhythm of your body rather than the things around you.

Continue following this pattern for the duration of your walk. As you move toward the end of your mindful body scan, slowly become more aware of your surroundings, and finish your walk by expressing gratitude. Be grateful for everything around you. For your body, and its ability to support you through your journey. Be grateful for each moment.

Visualization meditation

No matter what kind of life you are currently living, you have the power to visualize a different life, a different reality. Visualizing a different and better life and refusing to allow contrary thoughts to enter your mind, will keep hope and expectations high, and will one day turn the things you visualize into reality."

~ Remez Sasson (Sasson, 2019)

We have all come across the term to visualize in the past. This involves being able to form clear pictures in your mind of exactly what it is that you want to achieve. It is often used by athletes for them to reach their goals. Before an event or competition, they use meditation to help them mentally see themselves winning. They use all of their faculties during meditation to get them there. Sight, sound, smell, touch, taste. A prominent practitioner of this form of meditation is the Olympic swimming gold medalist, Michael Phelps.

Preparation Before You Begin

For ease of repetition, get yourself into the right environment. Decide whether you are going to use seated or lying down meditation because you need to close your eyes for visualization. For this meditation we are going to help you find that place you can go to whenever you are feeling stressed out or anxious. In other words, your "happy place."

Breathing

Follow the first few steps we've already mentioned in previous guided meditations to calm yourself and get in tune with your body through breathing. Use the technique that works best for you.

Beginning of Your Visualization Meditation

Imagine somewhere you have either been before or somewhere you may want to be. It should be somewhere peaceful.

Use your sight, touch, smell, sound, and taste to expand this vision. Look around you.

Check in with Your Body

What can you see? Focus on the details.

If there happen to be mountains surrounding a lake, how high are the mountains?

What colors are they?

What time of the day is it?

Is the lake calm?

Is there a breeze blowing?

What can you smell?

Is there freshness coming off the water?

Is there a slight mist resting gently on the water, as the sun rises over the mountains?

Can you feel the sunlight as it bathes your skin?

What does it feel like?

Is the sky filled with clouds slowly drifting by, or is it a clear blue?

Look around the lake. Are there jetty's allowing you to walk out, sit down, and take it all in?

Can you see any boats on the lake?

Are there other people around? Maybe an early morning fisherman.

Move as far into your vision as possible. Begin to enjoy the peace and serenity of the moment. As you experience the wonder of nature. Of peace and tranquility.

With each breath you take, breathe in the peace you are feeling. Breathe it in deeply, slowly, feel the tranquility as each breath fills your lungs. As you exhale slowly, release all tension you may be feeling together with this breath. Let go of any negative emotions. Allow toxic thoughts to leave your body.

Breathe in calm, peace, serenity, and hope, while you breathe out all the negativity that is holding you back. Breathe in vital energy. Breathe out debilitating exhaustion and frustration. Breathe in happiness, contentment, and excitement. Breathe out stress, anxiety, and self-doubt.

Closing Your Meditation

Once you feel calmer and more confident, slowly begin to return to reality. Open your eyes, express gratitude for the meditative experience.

You now have another way to calm a busy mind. Deal with visualization to help you overcome fear, anger, tension, exhaustion, self-doubt, frustration, negativity, and any other bad feeling you may be experiencing. Return here often. It doesn't need to be the same place you always go to, but the technique and practice is the same. When just starting out, go to the same spot. Each time you go there, look for something new but remember your purpose is to meet your main aim—to become calm through visualization.

Sleep meditation

"Take a deep breath, relax and let go of your worries. Let the soothing essence of the night permeate and cleanse your entire being, slowly drawing you into deep relaxing slumber."

~ Unknown (Mani, 2019)

The main reason for practicing sleep meditation is so you can enjoy the benefits of a good night's rest. There is more to sleep than simply closing your eyes for the number of hours recommended by science. For many, sleep may eventually come but it is not peaceful. Inability to switch off the mind prevents us from truly being able to rest. This is one of the reasons for tossing and turning. Sleeping for short intervals and waking through the night. The following meditation will help with this and help you create the best environment for quality sleep, rather than quantity.

Restlessness, and an overactive mind are some of the main reasons sleep eludes us. Lack of sleep negatively impacts our health. Anything from increased risk of heart disease, chronic disease, delayed reaction time, and poor memory retention and problems making decisions. Insufficient rest can severely impact the body's ability to function efficiently.

Choosing to meditate before you retire to bed will improve your quality sleep. Not only can it help you relax and fall asleep quicker but you will also be able to sleep longer (if you battle with disturbed sleep.)

Believe it or not, being able to fall asleep has a lot to do with how relaxed our minds are. This begins with being able to get your thoughts under control during the day. Becoming mindful rather than allowing your mind to race. Clarity of thought throughout the day can lead to better sleep at night.

Preparation Before You Begin

Begin this meditation lying down on your bed, make sure you are ready for sleep and are comfortable in a resting position, you have done your bedtime routine tasks and are ready for sleep.

Breathing

Moderate your breathing by being mindful as you inhale and exhale. Use the breathing technique from earlier. You can count your breaths with the aim to slow your breathing. As you do so, notice how your body begins to feel more relaxed.

Check in with Your Body

Take note of each part of your body. When it comes to scanning each part beginning at your toes, moving upward, be mindful of what each feels like. Notice whether you are feeling light or weighed down. The main aim should be to relax each part of the body, do you feel the contact points between your relaxed body and the bed, can you feel yourself sinking into the soft mattress. To relax muscles, become mindful of any pain you may feel. Tension you may be holding onto. Release each of these so you can relax, ready to drift off into a deep sleep.

Visualizing a beautiful peaceful place can get you into that calm space. Making it easier for you to drift off without having a million thoughts running through your mind. Include things like gratitude as part of the visualization process.

Closing Your Meditation

We've covered counting your breathing. Counting can also assist you in quieting your mind by focusing on the numeric order whether counting forward or backward. You are focusing your thoughts and channeling your consciousness by focusing on something else, rather than the busyness of the day.

If you happen to have a restless night's sleep you can consider focused breathing again, combined with a scan throughout your body searching for areas that need to be relaxed. Count each breath as you inhale over two counts. Hold the breath for a count of three, and exhale counting to four. Repeat each breath cycle ten times. By this time, you should be feeling way more relaxed and ready to return to a restful sleep.

NOTES

_____
_____

_____
_____

_____
_____

Conclusion

"The things that matter most in our lives are not fantastic or grand. They are moments when we touch one another."

~ Jack Kornfield (Selva, 2019)

What a wonderful place to find yourself. Fearless, free, and in touch with who you really are on the deepest level possible.

From the ancient Chinese, Buddhists, and other religions in the Middle East, mindfulness and meditation techniques have been around for thousands of years BCE. While they may have had their own stresses and challenges to deal with. If ever there has been a time in the history of the world for a means of being able to de-stress and calm a busy mind it is now. The way to do this lies in the secrets of these past techniques.

Most of these techniques have only become popular in the western world over the last couple of decades. Despite this, it was quickly discovered how both techniques complement each other, making it easier to cope with the busyness and demands of modern-day life. Now more than ever before it is important to find coping mechanisms that work. Ways to reduce stress, help you become mindful of what's going on around you and within you.

There are way too many mental, physical, and spiritual benefits to mention, however, it's safe to say that scientific evidence has proved that developing these skills can reduce stress, anxiety, possibly keeping depression and other mental health illnesses at bay because you know how to unwind and release the tension you may be feeling.

Health benefits include being able to lower your blood pressure, minimizing heart disease. Preventing you from toxic stress. Chronic pain can be reduced to manageable levels while a long list of physical conditions can be treated using some of these techniques.

We need to move beyond the past by learning to let go. Mindfulness can help you live in the present and be aware of each moment as it passes us by. The secret is not getting caught up in the moment. Not stressing about a future that has still not and may never happen. Instead, discover how to live from one moment to the next.

By now you would have realized that there is way more to meditation and being mindful than sitting with your legs crossed, finger touching your thumb and chanting in an ancient language. Of course, if this is the way that you, personally find your way to getting in touch with yourself and tapping into your consciousness then by all means. You've made it work for you.

That however is the message of this book. It's learning the reasons behind why you should be doing these things, what some of the benefits are that you can immediately begin to apply to your life, and how to apply them. Part of the process is finding what works for you and then using that consistently. That's right. You need to choose to make the time for yourself. Don't see it as a sacrifice because it is really an investment. An investment in you discovering who you are. Discovering inner peace. Guided meditation can help you get there without joining any groups or paying exorbitant fees on equipment. All you need is yourself and a suitable quiet space to clear your mind.

Remember that guided meditation and mindfulness don't need to be complicated. There are way more benefits in being able to apply these things to your life daily. The exciting thing is that as you enjoy each of the benefits, those around you enjoy them too. Your ability to calm your thoughts and your mind can relieve unnecessary tension. It can make you more tolerant of those around you. You can make wiser decisions that will impact the lives of those you associate with, whether in your home or work environments. In short, others will find it easier to get along with you because you will be more relaxed and at peace with yourself.

In the chapter above there are a number of techniques that you can use for guided meditations. These are just a handful of ways you can access your inner being. That you can calm and heal yourself from the inside out. Ways that you can improve your life, simply beginning with breathing techniques. We all breathe, right? The secret to meditation and mindfulness however is learning to breathe correctly and being able to apply this anytime you need to. It is knowing exactly what to do and then tailoring the basics to be applied in any meditation.

While only a handful are mentioned there are way more guided meditations available to you. The most important part of *Meditation & Mindfulness* however is discovering who you are, and the best ways that these practices can benefit you in your life. How they can help you strengthen relationships, control your own emotions, understand the emotions of others, and access that happy place whenever you need it, and boy, do we often need it!

As an author, it is extremely important for me to receive feedback from my readers. This not only helps me become a better writer, but it also gives me the opportunity of being able to share this work to benefit those that need it most.

If you have found this book of value and enjoyed the content, please leave a comment in the comment section below or on the platform where you made the purchase. Thank you in advance.

Namaste!

How did you enjoy reading Meditation & Mindfulness?

I want to say thank you for purchasing and reading this book! I really hope you enjoyed it and it's provided value to your life.

If you enjoyed reading this book and found some benefit in it, I'd love your support and hope that you could take a moment to post a review on Amazon. I'd love to hear from you, even if you have feedback, as it'll help me in ensuring that I improve this book and others in the future.

To leave your Amazon review, I've made it as easy as possible for you. Just make a note of the below link or visit your account where you purchased the book to write a review:

Here is the link to leave your Amazon review: https://www.amazon.co.uk/review/create-review/?channel=glance-detail&asin=B0BBXNP8DY&ie=UTF8

I want to let you know that your review is very important to me and will help this book reach and impact more people's lives.

Thanks for your time and support.

Noah

Resources

Following is a list of additional resources that you may find useful on your journey toward peace and enlightenment. This list is by no means exhaustive and should rather be seen as a recommended starting point. There are also a couple of apps that you may want to check out. Each of these will give you access to thousands of guided meditations for you to add to your arsenal.

As a Man Thinketh by James Allen

Authentic Happiness: Using the new positive psychology to realize your potential for lasting fulfillment by Martin E. P. Seligman

Emotional Intelligence: Why it can matter more than IQ by Daniel Goleman

How to Stop Worrying and Start Living by Dale Carnegie

Outliers by Malcolm Gladwell

The Alchemist by Paulo Coelho

The Four Agreements: A practical guide to personal freedom by Miguel Ruiz

The Happiness Hypothesis by Jonathan Heidt

The Monk Who Sold His Ferrari by Robin Sharma

The Power of Now: A guide to spiritual enlightenment by Eckhart Tolle

The Richest Man in Babylon by George S. Clason

The Secret by Rhonda Byrne

Think and Grow Rich by Napoleon Hill

Thinking Fast and Slow by Daniel Kahneman

Wherever You Go, There You Are by Jon Kabat-Zinn

Full Catastrophe Living by Jon Kabat-Zinn

Practicing the Presence of God by Brother Lawrence

Being Peace by Thich Nhat Hanh

Peace is Every Step by Thich Nhat Hanh

The Unexpected Power of Mindfulness and Meditation by Ed Shapiro & Deb Shapiro

Headspace – https://www.headspace.com

Calm – https://www.calm.com

Insight timer – https://insightimer.com

Simple Habit – https://www.simplehabit.com

Buddhify - https://buddhify.com/

References

Ackerman, C. (2018, July 25). *What is Neuroplasticity? A Psychologist Explains [+14 Exercises]*. PositivePsychology.com. https://positivepsychology.com/neuroplasticity/

Ackerman, C. E. (2019, July 10). *23 Amazing Health Benefits of Mindfulness for Body and Brain*. PositivePsychology.com. https://positivepsychology.com/benefits-of-mindfulness/

Allen, J. (2019). *As A Man Thinketh*. Indo European Publishing Co.

American Psychological Association. (2020, October). *Stress in America 2020*. Apa.org; American Psychological Association. https://www.apa.org/news/press/releases/stress/2020/report-october

Ankrom, S. (2022, February 14). *8 Deep Breathing Exercises for Anxiety*. Verywell Mind. https://www.verywellmind.com/abdominal-breathing-2584115

Babauta, L. (2016). *Meditation for Beginners: 20 Practical tips for understanding the mind*. Zenhabits.net. https://zenhabits.net/meditation-guide/

Basso, Dr. J. C. (n.d.). *6 Reasons You Should Incorporate Meditation Into Your Daily Routine*. Thriveglobal.com.

https://thriveglobal.com/stories/reasons-to-include-meditation-in-daily-routine/

Bertin, M. (2015, November 9). *Mindfulness Meditation: Guided practices*. Mindful. https://www.mindful.org/mindfulness-meditation-guided-practices/

Bhasin, M. K., Dusek, J. A., Chang, B.-H., Joseph, M. G., Denninger, J. W., Fricchione, G. L., Benson, H., & Libermann, T. A. (2013). Relaxation Response Induces Temporal Transcriptome Changes in Energy Metabolism, Insulin Secretion and Inflammatory Pathways. *PLoS ONE, 8*(5), e62817. https://doi.org/10.1371/journal.pone.0062817

Booth, R. (2017, October 22). Master of mindfulness. *The Guardian*. https://www.theguardian.com/lifeandstyle/2017/oct/22/mindfulness-jon-kabat-zinn-depression-trump-grenfell

Borys, A. (2013, August 12). *What is Advanced Meditation Like?* Www.newworldlibrary.com. https://www.newworldlibrary.com/Blog/tabid/767/articleld/174/What-is-Advanced-Meditation-Like-by-guest-blogger-Ajayan-Borys.aspx#.YtA94qTRayM

Brady, A. (2019, August 18). *4 Advanced Meditation Techniques and Tools to Deepen Your Practice*. Chopra. https://chopra.com/articles/4-advanced-meditation-techniques-and-tools-to-deepen-your-practice

Buddhify. (2020). Buddhify. https://buddhify.com/

Burgs. (2021, December 4). *What Are the Four Phases of Meditation? (Advanced)*. The Art of Meditation. https://theartofmeditation.org/burgs-blog/the-four-phases-of-meditation-advanced

Byrne, R. (2016). *The secret : the 10th anniversary edition.* Atria Books ; Hillsboro, Or.

Carnegie, D. (2019). *How To Stop Worrying And Start Living.* Jaico Publishing House.

Cassata, C. (2021, June 8). *10 Areas That Mindfulness & Meditation Make Us Better*. Psych Central. https://psychcentral.com/blog/surprising-health-benefits-of-mindfulness-meditation

Celes. (2009, April 27). *10 Reasons You Should Meditate.* Personal Excellence. https://personalexcellence.co/blog/reasons-to-meditate/

Cherry, K. (2021, October 15). *Benefits of Mindfulness.* Verywell Mind. https://www.verywellmind.com/the-benefits-of-mindfulness-5205137

Cherry, K. (2022, February 22). *What is Mindfulness Meditation?* Verywell Mind; Verywellmind. https://www.verywellmind.com/mindfulness-meditation-88369

Chow, S. (2018, August 23). *Meditation History.* News-Medical.net. https://www.news-medical.net/health/Meditation-History.aspx

Clason, G. S. (2018). *Richest Man In Babylon.*

Cleveland Clinic. (2019). *Diaphragmatic Breathing*. Cleveland Clinic. https://my.clevelandclinic.org/health/articles/9445-diaphragmatic-breathing

Coelho, P. (1988). *The Alchemist*. New York Harpercollins Publishers.

Cohut, M. (2019, March 29). *What does science say about the effects of meditation?* Www.medicalnewstoday.com. https://www.medicalnewstoday.com/articles/324839

Contributor. (2019, January 17). *The 4 Basic Stages of Meditation: And their relationship with Patanjali's 8 limbs of Yoga*. The Mindful Word. https://www.themindfulword.org/2019/stages-of-meditation-yoga/

Contributors. (2004, September). *Dhāraṇā*. Wikipedia.org; Wikimedia Foundation, Inc. https://en.m.wikipedia.org/wiki/Dh%C4%81ra%E1%B9%87%C4%81

Cronkleton, E. (2019, April 9). *10 Breathing Techniques for Stress Relief and More*. Healthline; Healthline Media. https://www.healthline.com/health/breathing-exercise

Crumpler, C. (2022, April 28). *What to know about body scan meditation*. Www.medicalnewstoday.com. https://www.medicalnewstoday.com/articles/body-scan-meditation

Cuncic, A. (2021, November 10). *How Do You Live in the Present?* Verywell Mind. https://www.verywellmind.com/how-do-you-live-in-the-present-5204439

Currin-Sheehan, K. (2021, June 9). *A Primer on Present Moment Awareness.* Psych Central. https://psychcentral.com/blog/how-to-do-present-moment-awareness-meditation

Daubenmier, J., Kristeller, J., Hecht, F. M., Maninger, N., Kuwata, M., Jhaveri, K., Lustig, R. H., Kemeny, M., Karan, L., & Epel, E. (2011). Mindfulness Intervention for Stress Eating to Reduce Cortisol and Abdominal Fat among Overweight and Obese Women: An Exploratory Randomized Controlled Study. *Journal of Obesity, 2011*, 1–13. https://doi.org/10.1155/2011/651936

Davis, D. M., & Hayes, J. A. (2012). What are the benefits of mindfulness? *Https://Www.apa.org.* https://www.apa.org/monitor/2012/07-08/ce-corner

Dharma Master Hwansan Sunim. (2017, December 6). *Breath Counting Meditation: How to build mental power.* HuffPost. https://www.huffpost.com/entry/breath-counting-meditation_b_9698598

Don Miguel Ruiz. (2008). *The Four Agreements.* Hay House Inc.

Eisler, M. (2019, August 27). *Explaining The Difference Between Mindfulness & Meditation.* Chopra.

https://chopra.com/articles/explaining-the-difference-between-mindfulness-meditation

Emma-Louise. (2021, October 8). *Relax Your Clients in Under 5 Minutes with these Guided Meditation Scripts*. The Coaching Tools Company. https://www.thecoachingtoolscompany.com/de-stress-series-relax-clients-in-under-5-mins-guided-meditation-scripts/

Essence of Humanity. (n.d.). *How Meditation and Mindfulness Can Improve Your Appearance*. Essence of Humanity. https://www.theessenceofhumanity.com/blogs/news/how-meditation-and-mindfulness-can-improve-your-appearance

Estrada, J. (2020, July 5). *Meditation Actually Encourages an Active Mind--Here's How It's Done*. Well+Good. https://www.wellandgood.com/visualization-meditation/

Experience Calm. (n.d.). Calm.com. https://calm.com

Famous Quotes & Sayings. (n.d.). *Top 55 Don't Make Use Of Me Quotes & Sayings*. Quotessayings.net. https://quotessayings.net/topics/dont-make-use-of-me/

Farrell, S. (2014, September 12). *The Beauty Benefits of Meditation*. Women's Health. https://www.womenshealthmag.com/beauty/a19941638/beauty-benefits-of-meditation/

Fletcher, E. (2015, September 10). *Why Meditation & Visualization Aren't The Same (And How To Use Them)*. Mindbodygreen. https://www.mindbodygreen.com/0-

21539/why-meditation-visualization-arent-the-same-and-how-to-use-them.html

Francis, C. A. (2019, December 30). *How to Be Happy by Living in the Present Moment*. Mindfulness Meditation Institute. https://mindfulnessmeditationinstitute.org/2019/12/30/how-to-be-happy-by-living-in-the-present-moment/

Friedel-Hunt, M. (2016, December 18). *Meditations for Grievers*. GriefHaven.org. https://griefhaven.org/meditations-for-grievers/

Ginexi, E., Burk Quinlan, E., & Shurtleff, D. (2022). *Meditation and Mindfulness: What you need to know*. NCCIH. https://www.nccih.nih.gov/health/meditation-and-mindfulness-what-you-need-to-know

Gladwell, M. (2008). *Outliers : the story of success*. Back Bay Books, Cop.

Gohel, J. (2014, January 16). *How Meditation Can Help to Improve Your Productivity*. Lifehack. https://www.lifehack.org/articles/productivity/how-meditation-can-help-improve-your-productivity.html

Goleman, D. (1996). *Emotional Intelligence: Why It Can Matter More than IQ*. Bloomsbury.

Good Reads. (n.d.-a). *A quote by James Baraz*. Www.goodreads.com. https://www.goodreads.com/quotes/232890

Good Reads. (n.d.-b). *A quote from Beautify your Breath - Beautify your Life.* Www.goodreads.com. https://www.goodreads.com/quotes/7482550

GoodTherapy.org Staff. (2018, July 1). *Let Go, Be Present: Quotes about mindfulness and meditation.* GoodTherapy.org Therapy Blog. https://www.goodtherapy.org/blog/let-go-be-present-quotes-about-mindfulness-and-meditation-0701187

Haidt, J. (2006). *The happiness hypothesis : putting ancient wisdom and philosophy to the test of modern science.* Arrow.

Harvard Health Publishing. (2016, March 10). *Learning diaphragmatic breathing.* Harvard Health. https://www.health.harvard.edu/healthbeat/learning-diaphragmatic-breathing

Hassan, M. (2019, May 2). *How to Meditate on Love.* Psych Central. https://psychcentral.com/blog/spirituality/2019/05/how-to-meditate-on-love

Headspace. (n.d.-a). *How does meditation improve relationships?* Www.headspace.com. https://www.headspace.com/articles/meditation-and-our-relationships-with-others

Headspace. (n.d.-b). *Short meditation.* Www.headspace.com. https://www.headspace.com/meditation/short-meditation

Headspace. (2014). *Meditation for Sleep.* Headspace. https://www.headspace.com/meditation/sleep

Headspace. (2016). *Visualization Meditation*. Headspace. https://www.headspace.com/meditation/visualization

Headspace. (2018). *How to relax*. Headspace. https://www.headspace.com/meditation/how-to-relax

Headspace. (2020a). *Types of Meditation*. Headspace. https://www.headspace.com/meditation/techniques

Headspace. (2020b). *Walking Meditation - Headspace*. Headspace. https://www.headspace.com/meditation/walking-meditation

Headspace. (2021). *33 of the Best Meditation Quotes*. Headspace. https://www.headspace.com/meditation/quotes

Hebshi-Holt, S. (2022, April 13). *9 Guided Meditation Scripts: Short + Long*. LoveToKnow. https://www.lovetoknowhealth.com/fitness/guided-meditation-script

Heckman, W. (2022, April 11). *Stress Level Of Americans Is Rising Rapidly In 2022, New Study Finds*. The American Institute of Stress. https://www.stress.org/stress-level-of-americans-is-rising-rapidly-in-2022-new-study-finds

Hill, N. (2019). *Think And Grow Rich*. Simon & Brown. (Original work published 1937)

Ho-My, G. C. (n.d.). *What Are The Origins Of Mindfulness?* Thriveglobal.com. https://thriveglobal.com/stories/what-are-the-origins-of-mindfulness/

Holland, E. (2016, December 14). *Alone Time: 4 reasons you need it and 4 ways to enjoy it*. Chopra.

https://chopra.com/articles/alone-time-4-reasons-you-need-it-and-4-ways-to-enjoy-it

Holland, E. (2019, May 17). *How to Cultivate Inner Strength Through Meditation.* Chopra. https://chopra.com/articles/how-to-cultivate-inner-strength-through-meditation

Inner IDEA. (2019). *Meditation 101: Techniques, Benefits, and a Beginner's How-to.* Gaiam. https://www.gaiam.com/blogs/discover/meditation-101-techniques-benefits-and-a-beginner-s-how-to

Inner Peace Fellowship Meditation. (n.d.). *How To Meditate.* Innerpeacefellowship.org. https://www.innerpeacefellowship.org/how-to-meditate/

Insight Network, Inc. (2021). *Insight Timer.* Insighttimer.com. https://insighttimer.com

Itani, O. (2020, January 29). *In Search of Solitude: The importance and benefits of spending time alone.* OMAR ITANI. https://www.omaritani.com/blog/spending-time-alone

Jaffe, D. (2018, August 20). *Working through illness and grief with meditation.* Buddhify. https://buddhify.com/working-through-illness-and-grief-with-meditation/

Jewell, T., & Hoshaw, C. (2021, November 5). *What is Diaphragmatic Breathing?* Healthline. https://www.healthline.com/health/diaphragmatic-breathing

Juma, N. (2022, June 15). *Jon Kabat-Zinn Quotes That Make Life Better*. Everyday Power. https://everydaypower.com/jon-kabat-zinn-quotes/

Kabat-Zinn, J. (2004). *Wherever you go, there you are*. Piatkus.

Kabat-Zinn, J. (2008). *Full catastrophe living*. Random House Audio.

Kabat-Zinn, J. (2019). *Mindfulness Definition | What Is Mindfulness?* Greater Good. https://greatergood.berkeley.edu/topic/mindfulness/definition

Kahneman, D. (2011). *Thinking, Fast and Slow*. Farrar, Straus And Giroux.

Kapanen, K. (2015, July 28). *Dharana: The 6th limb of yoga explained*. DoYou. https://www.doyou.com/dharana-the-6th-limb-of-yoga-explained-38938/

Larkin, E. (2020, October 25). *How to create a daily routine that works for you*. The Spruce. https://www.thespruce.com/how-to-create-a-daily-routine-2648007

Lawrence, B. (2018). *Practicing The Presence Of God*.

Lazar, S. W., Kerr, C. E., Wasserman, R. H., Gray, J. R., Greve, D. N., Treadway, M. T., McGarvey, M., Quinn, B. T., Dusek, J. A., Benson, H., Rauch, S. L., Moore, C. I., & Fischl, B. (2005). Meditation experience is associated with increased cortical thickness. *Neuroreport, 16*(17), 1893–1897. https://doi.org/10.1097/01.wnr.0000186598.66243.19

Legace, M. (2019, February 8). *100 Meditation Quotes (for less stress and more calmness)*. WisdomQuotes. https://wisdomquotes.com/meditation-quotes/

Leonard, A. (2020, July 31). *Root to Rise: Following the history of mindfulness back to its source*. Www.blinkist.com. https://www.blinkist.com/magazine/posts/history-of-mindfulness

Lindberg, S. (2020, January 16). *Is There a Best Time of Day to Meditate?* Healthline. https://www.healthline.com/health/mental-health/best-time-to-meditate

Majsiak, B., & Young, C. (2022, June 23). *7 Ways to Practice Breath Work for Beginners*. EverydayHealth.com. https://www.everydayhealth.com/alternative-health/living-with/ways-practice-breath-focused-meditation/

Mani, M. (2019, January 24). *15 Soothing Quotes To Help You Sleep (With Relaxing Pictures)*. OutofStress.com. https://www.outofstress.com/soothing-quotes-for-sleep/

Martine, C. A. (2019, August 11). *Find Yourself quote*. Medium. https://medium.com/@christyannmartine/find-yourself-88b9af7711dc

Martinez, Dr. N. (2021). *105 Mindfulness Quotes for Work, Life, and Love*. Everydaypower.com. https://everydaypower.com/mindfulness-quotes-work-life-love

Matejko, S. (2022, June 13). *What's the Background of Mindfulness?* Psych Central. https://psychcentral.com/lib/a-brief-history-of-mindfulness-in-the-usa-and-its-impact-on-our-lives

Mayo Clinic staff. (2020, April 22). *Meditation: A simple, fast way to reduce stress.* Mayo Clinic. https://www.mayoclinic.org/tests-procedures/meditation/in-depth/meditation/art-20045858

McCumiskey, C. (2019, February 19). *The benefits of meditation.* Spiritual Heart. https://spiritualearth.com/benefits-of-meditation/

Mead, E. (2019, July 4). *The History and Origin of Meditation.* PositivePsychology.com. https://positivepsychology.com/history-of-meditation/

Meditation and Sleep Made Simple - Headspace. (2017). Headspace. https://www.headspace.com

Mendel, B. (2021, February 14). *Discovering Genuine Confidence through Meditation.* Mindworks Meditation. https://mindworks.org/blog/discovering-genuine-confidence-meditation/

Merriam-Webster Dictionary. (2019). *Definition of MINDFULNESS.* Merriam-Webster.com. https://www.merriam-webster.com/dictionary/mindfulness

Mindful. (2021, March 8). *10 Guided Meditations from the Powerful Women of the Mindfulness Movement.* Mindful.

https://www.mindful.org/guided-meditations-from-the-powerful-women-of-the-mindfulness-movement/

Mindful Staff. (2019, October 18). *Mindfulness: How to do it*. Mindful. https://www.mindful.org/mindfulness-how-to-do-it/

Mindworks Team. (2017a, June 23). *Meditation and Breathing Techniques*. Mindworks Meditation. https://mindworks.org/blog/breathing-techniques-meditation/

Mindworks Team. (2017b, August 16). *Falling Asleep During Guided Meditation | What to Do When You Meditate*. Mindworks Meditation. https://mindworks.org/blog/falling-asleep-during-guided-meditation/

Mindworks Team. (2017c, October 16). *Focus Meditation: How to improve memory & focus*. Mindworks Meditation. https://mindworks.org/blog/focus-meditation/

Mindworks Team. (2017d, November 9). *The 5 Essential Points of Meditation*. Mindworks Meditation; Mindworks Meditation. https://mindworks.org/blog/5-essential-points-of-meditation/

Mindworks Team. (2019a, August 22). *Patience is Power*. Mindworks Meditation. https://mindworks.org/blog/patience-is-power/

Mindworks Team. (2019b, October 20). *When Is the Best Time of Day to Meditate?* Mindworks Meditation. https://mindworks.org/blog/when-is-the-best-time-of-day-to-meditate/

Mindworks Team. (2021, January 25). *Why is Meditation Important? 6 Facts You Need to Know*. Mindworks Meditation. https://mindworks.org/blog/why-is-meditation-important-facts-you-need-to-know

MITM. (2021, March 17). *10 Awesome Benefits of Guided Meditation.* MIND IS the MASTER. https://mindisthemaster.com/benefits-of-guided-meditation/

Moore, C. (2019, April 9). *What Is Mindfulness? Definition + Benefits (Incl. Psychology)*. PositivePsychology.com. https://positivepsychology.com/what-is-mindfulness/

Morin, A. (2020, February 11). *How to Get Started With Guided Meditation.* Verywell Mind. https://www.verywellmind.com/guided-meditation-getting-started-4174283

Murphy, A. (2020, December 1). *History of Meditation: The origin story of meditating.* Declutter the Mind. https://declutterthemind.com/blog/history-of-meditation/

My Self Love Supply. (2021, April 4). *Why Meditation Should Be a Part of Your Daily Routine!* My Self-Love Supply. https://myselflovesupply.com/blogs/blog/why-meditation-should-be-a-part-of-your-daily-routine

Nash, J. (2022, June 19). *How to Practice Visualization Meditation: 3 best scripts.* PositivePsychology.com. https://positivepsychology.com/visualization-meditation/

Nast, C. (2020, September 1). *How to Meditate When You Have No Idea Where to Start.* SELF. https://www.self.com/story/how-to-meditate

Nhất Hạnh, Thích. (2008). *Being peace.* Read How You Want.

Nhất Hạnh, Thích. (2013). *Peace is Every Step.* Bantam/Ajp.

Northwestern Medicine Staff. (2016, August 15). *Health Benefits of Having a Routine.* Northwestern Medicine; Northwestern Medicine. https://www.nm.org/healthbeat/healthy-tips/health-benefits-of-having-a-routine

Nunez, K. (2020, January 13). *Meditation for Sleep: How to use meditation for insomnia, better sleep.* Healthline. https://www.healthline.com/health/meditation-for-sleep

Okafor, J. (2022, June 24). *History of Mindfulness, From East to West to Mainstream.* TRVST. https://www.trvst.world/mind-body/history-of-mindfulness/

Ong, J. C., Manber, R., Segal, Z., Xia, Y., Shapiro, S., & Wyatt, J. K. (2014). A randomized controlled trial of mindfulness meditation for chronic insomnia. *Sleep, 37*(9), 1553–1563. https://doi.org/10.5665/sleep.4010

Parade. (2020, April 16). *The Compassion Connection: How meditating for the good of others will benefit you as well.* Parade: Entertainment, Recipes, Health, Life, Holidays. https://parade.com/717338/parade/the-compassion-connection-how-meditating-for-the-good-of-others-will-benefit-you-as-well/

Powell, A. (2018, April 9). *Harvard researchers study how mindfulness may change the brain in depressed patients.* Harvard Gazette. https://news.harvard.edu/gazette/story/2018/04/harvard-researchers-study-how-mindfulness-may-change-the-brain-in-depressed-patients/

Puddicombe, A. (n.d.). *Can I apply mindfulness to driving?* Www.headspace.com. https://www.headspace.com/articles/applying-mindfulness-to-driving

Puff PhD, R. (2013). *An Overview of Meditation: Its Origins and Traditions.* Psychology Today. https://www.psychologytoday.com/us/blog/meditation-modern-life/201307/overview-meditation-its-origins-and-traditions

Raypole, C. (2020a, March 26). *How to Do a Body Scan Meditation (and Why You Should).* Healthline. https://www.healthline.com/health/body-scan-meditation

Raypole, C. (2020b, May 28). *5 Visualization Techniques to Add to Your Meditation Practice.* Healthline. https://www.healthline.com/health/visualization-meditation

Raypole, C. (2020c, September 27). *The Beginner's Guide to Mirror Gazing Meditation.* Healthline.

https://www.healtline.com/health/mental-health/mirror-gazing

Rinzler, L. (2016, May 24). *A Breath Meditation for Intermediate Practitioners.* Sonima. https://www.sonima.com/meditation/intermediate-meditation/

Robbins, M. (2017). *The 5 second rule : transform your life, work, and confidence with everyday courage.* Savio Republic.

Ross, A. (2016, March 9). *How Meditation Went Mainstream.* Time; Time. https://time.com/4246928/meditation-history-buddhism/

Sara, J. (2020, January 2). *7 Ways Meditation Cultivates Inner Strength and Grit.* Yoga Basics. https://www.yogabasics.com/connect/yoga-blog/meditation-cultivates-inner-strength-grit/

Sasson, R. (2019, October 21). *Creative Visualization Quotes for Creating Positive Changes.* Success Consciousness. https://www.successconsciousness.com/blog/quotes/creative-visualization-quotes/

Scott, E. (2020, June 11). *What is Mindfulness?* Verywell Mind. https://www.verywellmind.com/mindfulness-the-health-and-stress-relief-benefits-3145189

Scott, E. (2021a, September 13). *Body Scan Meditation: Release tension with this targeted meditation technique.*

Verywell Mind. https://www.verywellmind.com/body-scan-meditation-why-and-how-3144782

Scott, E. (2021b, September 19). *Focused Meditation: How to start a practice.* Verywell Mind. https://www.verywellmind.com/practice-focused-meditation-3144785

Seligman, M. E. P. (2002). *Authentic happiness : using the new positive psychology to realize your potential for lasting fulfilment.* Nicholas Brealey Publishing.

Selva, J. (2017, March 13). *History of Mindfulness: from East to West and religion to science.* PositivePsychology.com. https://positivepsychology.com/history-of-mindfulness/

Selva, J. (2019, July 4). *76 Most Powerful Mindfulness Quotes: Your daily dose of inspiration.* PositivePsychology.com. https://positivepsychology.com/mindfulness-quotes/

Shapiro, D., & Shapiro, E. (2019). *The Unexpected Power of Mindfulness and Meditation.* Ixia Press.

Shapiro, E., & Shapiro, D. (2017, May 8). *The Difference Between Mindfulness and Meditation.* Medium; Thrive Global. https://medium.com/thrive-global/mindfulness-meditation-whats-the-difference-852f5ef7ec1a

Sharma, R. (2014, October 11). *Learn to Meditate.* The New Indian Express.

https://www.newindianexpress.com/cities/bengaluru/2014/oct/11/Learn-to-Meditate-670253.html

Sharma, R. S. (2012). *The monk who sold his Ferrari : a remarkable story about living your dreams.* Harpercollins Canada.

Shaw, A. (2019, September 19). *Meditation For Anxious Overthinkers.* Ascent Publication. https://medium.com/the-ascent/meditation-for-anxious-overthinkers-3e05f2fbbd71

Simon, S. (2021, November 29). *How to Practice Mindfulness the Right Way.* Verywell Health. https://www.verywellhealth.com/mindfulness-study-practice-5210428

Simple Habit | The Best Meditation App for Busy People. (n.d.). Simplehabit.com. https://simplehabit.com

Smith, J. A., Newman, K. M., Suttie, J., & Jazaieri, H. (2017, December 5). *The State of Mindfulness Science.* Greater Good. https://greatergood.berkeley.edu/article/item/the_state_of_mindfulness_science

Stokes, V. (2021, April 12). *Spiritual Meditation: What it is, benefits, and how to practice.* Healthline. https://www.healthline.com/health/mind-body/spiritual-meditation

Suthers, J. (2014, September 12). *How to Meditate - Final Part: Advanced meditation technique.* Sage Meditation.

https://www.sagemeditation.com/how-to-meditate-advanced-meditation-technique/

Suttie, J. (2018, October 29). *Five science-backed reasons mindfulness meditation is good for your health.* Mindful. https://www.mindful.org/five-ways-mindfulness-meditation-is-good-for-your-health/

Tassone, S. A. (2012, February 6). *The Seven Stages of a Lay Meditator.* Www.psychologytoday.com. https://www.psychologytoday.com/us/blog/the-90-minute-checkup/201202/the-seven-stages-lay-meditator

Team, M. (2017, August 29). *How to Meditate for Better Concentration.* Mindworks Meditation. https://mindworks.org/blog/how-meditate-better-concentration/

The Art of Living. (2020). *Here's how you can have better decision-making abilities.* Art of Living (Global). https://www.artofliving.org/meditation/meditation-for-you/meditation-for-better-decision-making

The Chopra.com Team. (2013, February 22). *Why Meditate?* Chopra. https://chopra.com/articles/why-meditate

The Editors at Chopra.com. (2018, August 28). *Top 30 Deepak Chopra Quotes.* Chopra. https://chopra.com/articles/top-30-deepak-chopra-quotes

Thorp, T. (2019, June 26). *How to Boost Your Confidence Through Meditation.* Chopra.

https://chopra.com/articles/how-to-boost-your-confidence-through-meditation

Thorpe, M., & Link, R. (2020, October 27). *12 Science-Based Benefits of Meditation*. Healthline. https://www.healthline.com/nutrition/12-benefits-of-meditation

Tolle, E. (2004). *The power of NOW : a guide to spiritual enlightenment*. Namaste Pub. ; Novato, Calif.

Vanessa Van Edwards. (2015, November 5). *14 Amazing Benefits of Meditation That Can Actually Rewire Your Brain*. Science of People; Science of People. https://www.scienceofpeople.com/meditation-benefits/

Varnum, H. (2021, July 10). *How to Create a Guided Meditation*. Guided Meditation Framework. https://guidedmeditationframework.com/blog/how-to-create-a-guided-meditation/

Vincenty, S. (2020, November 21). *How to Find Inner Peace and Happiness in the Chaos*. Oprah Daily. https://www.oprahdaily.com/life/a29474453/how-to-find-inner-peace/

Vishnubhotla, R. V., Radhakrishnan, R., Kveraga, K., Deardorff, R., Ram, C., Pawale, D., Wu, Y.-C., Renschler, J., Subramaniam, B., & Sadhasivam, S. (2021). Advanced Meditation Alters Resting-State Brain Network Connectivity Correlating With Improved Mindfulness. *Frontiers in Psychology, 12*. https://doi.org/10.3389/fpsyg.2021.745344

Wagner, P. (2019, December 4). *Meditation and Mindfulness; Methods for lasting peace*. Gaia. https://www.gaia.com/article/meditation-vs-mindfulness-methods-mindsets-for-lasting-peace

Walton, A. G. (2018, January 17). 7 Ways Meditation Can Actually Change The Brain. *Forbes*. https://www.forbes.com/sites/alicegwalton/2015/02/09/7-ways-meditation-can-actually-change-the-brain/

Wanderlust. (2018, June 13). *Top 10 Reasons to Meditate*. Mindful. https://www.mindful.org/top-10-reasons-to-meditate/

Wellness Creative Co. (2021, May 12). *50+ Meditation Quotes Ideal For Stress, Mindfulness & Yoga*. Wellness Creative Co. https://www.wellnesscreatives.com/meditation-quotes

Yogapedia. (n.d.-a). *What is Dhyana? - Definition from Yogapedia*. Yogapedia.com. https://www.yogapedia.com/definition/5284/dhyana

Yogapedia. (n.d.-b). *What is Samadhi? - Definition from Yogapedia*. Yogapedia.com. https://yogapedia.com/definition/4995/samadhi

Zeidan, F., Grant, J. A., Brown, C. A., McHaffie, J. G., & Coghill, R. C. (2012). Mindfulness meditation-related pain relief: Evidence for unique brain mechanisms in the regulation of pain. *Neuroscience Letters*, *520*(2), 165–173. https://doi.org/10.1016/j.neulet.2012.03.082

Printed in Great Britain
by Amazon